Résistance
A Pascale Hervé Story
Mark Ellott

Mark Ellott Books

Résistance

(A Pascale Hervé Story)

by Mark Ellott

© 2025 Mark Ellott. All Rights Reserved.

First published in 2025 by Mark Ellott Books

While some historical characters and events are mentioned, the story, main characters, and situations in this book are entirely imaginary and have no relation to any real person or actual happenings.

The book is sold subject to the condition that it shall not, by way of trade or otherwise, be lent, re-sold, hired out or otherwise circulated without the publisher's prior consent in any form of binding or cover other than that in which it is published and without a similar condition including this condition being imposed on the subsequent purchaser.

No part of this publication may be reproduced or transmitted in any form or by any means, electronically or mechanically, including photocopying, recording or any information storage or retrieval system, without either the prior permission in writing from the publisher or a licence, permitted restricted copying.

MARK ELLOTT
BOOKS

http://www.ellott.co.uk

Cover image © 2025 Maire Ellott.

Also by Mark Ellott

The Pascale Hervé Detective Stories
Resolution
Recovery
Résistance

Contemporary Thrillers
Ransom

The Golden Age of Piracy
Renegade
Rose

Historical
Rebellion
Reiver

Short Story Collections
Blackjack
A Moment In Time
Raven and Other Stories
Sinistré, The Morning Cloud Chromicles

Author's Note

This portrayal of the French Resistance during the Second World War strives for historical accuracy, although some creative liberties have been taken for dramatic effect.

The Kulturverein für Heimkehr, for instance, is a fictional organisation, inspired by real groups that existed in the Weimar Republic to support the repatriation of ethnic Germans living abroad. I have made every effort to ensure that weapons, aircraft, vehicles, locations, and timelines are as accurate as possible. However, I apologise for any remaining errors or inconsistencies.

Thank you for joining me on this journey into a dark, complex, and often heroic chapter of history.

Mark Ellott, *May 2025*

Dramatis Personae

The Team – Present Day

Pascale Hervé: Co-owner of the Laurent Detective Agency; lead investigator.

Patrice Laurent: Pascale's husband and business partner.

Clarice Gunthier: The agency's technical expert.

David Radfield: Retired Detective Chief Inspector; now a team member and investigator.

Laurence Gunthier: Clarice's mother; Radfield's romantic partner.

Capitaine François Viala: Police Nationale officer; former colleague of Patrice and Pascale.

Other Characters – Present Day

Lucien Defrense: Son of Henri Defrense and nephew of Jean-Luc; researching his family history.

Yvonne Saunders: Archivist at the National Archives, London.

Ingrid Keller: Archivist at the Bundesarchiv, Berlin.

Geoffrey Spencer: MI6 director, historical records.

Maggie Blunt: MI6 supervisor.

Artur Giraud aka René Fournier: Son of André and Marguerite

1940s – England, Germany, and Occupied France

Claire Lemoine: Code name: Flamme – Language teacher turned SOE operative and resistance member.

Arthur Spencer: SOE recruiter and handler for Claire and James Kerr.

Jean-Luc Defrense: Code name: Mistral – Resistance operative; brother of Henri, uncle to Lucien.

Henri Defrense: Code name: Renaud – Resistance fighter; brother of Jean-Luc, father to Lucien.

Simone Berthier: Code name: Vigneron – Resistance fighter; fiancée of Jacques Morel.

Suzanne Moreau: Code name: Alouette – Resistance fighter; wife of Pierre Moreau.

Pierre Moreau: Forger and member of the resistance; husband of Suzanne.

Jacques Morel: Code name: Matelot – Resistance fighter; engaged to Simone Berthier.

Anton Marchand: Code name: Orage – Resistance fighter and saboteur.

André Fournier: Code name: Aigle – Resistance member; former soldier and owner of the Café Lys Noir.

Marguerite Fournier: Code name: Églantine – André's wife and co-owner of the Café Lys Noir; resistance member.

René Fournier: Son of André and Marguerite

James Kerr: Aliases: James Krüger, Vanguard – SOE operative.

Otto Reinhardt: German Great War veteran; recruiter for the Kulturverein für Heimkehr during the Weimar Republic.

Obersturmführer Franz Richter: SS Officer in charge of occupied Rouen

Untersturmführer Heinrich Vogel: SS officer, second in command to Franz Richter

Klaus Falkenrath: Gestapo officer who frequents the Café Lys Noir.

Prologue

July 1943, somewhere over France.

The Mosquito flew low in the dark sky, below the cloud cover. One engine was dead, and the other was failing, sputtering and misfiring, but just about keeping the machine in the air.

Flight Lieutenant Edward "Eddie" Hargrove gripped the yoke, fighting the machine to keep it in the air, his eyes darting between the flickering instruments and the darkened landscape below. He wondered how much longer he could keep the damaged aircraft limping along before he'd be forced to ditch, and if he did decide on the latter, it would be better here than at sea. Several days in a dinghy in the Channel, wondering if they would be picked up by friend or foe, didn't fill him with hope. Ditching on land offered a better proposition, but not least, there was no seasickness.

He glanced at his navigator. The man spoke passable French, so if they could make contact with partisans, they had a fighting chance of getting back to Blighty. Land it was, he decided, should he be unable to keep the kite aloft. Smoke coiled from the starboard nacelle, vanishing into the night. The prop moved lazily in the airstream.

"Where are we, Charlie?" He said to his navigator.

Flying Officer Charles "Charlie" Sinclair glanced at his charts. "Rouen should be just ahead." He squinted through the cockpit glass. "There it is." He paused, and then his voice tightened. "We've got company. Seven o'clock."

Eddie's stomach clenched. He turned his head, catching the silhouette of an ME109 closing fast. "I see him. Damn it. Looks like we will be ditching here. She won't survive this one."

The Messerschmitt fired. Tracer rounds streaked past. Metal shrieked as bullets tore through the fuselage. Eddie hauled at the controls, feeling the aircraft's sluggish response. "We're sitting ducks."

Charlie watched as flames flickered across the port engine. "We're on fire, Flight."

Eddie swore. They were too low to bail. No choice but to take their chances on the ground now.

"Damn."

Eddie pulled at the controls, turning the aircraft to starboard, feeling the resistance from the dead engine in his hands. He aimed for a field he could just about see beyond a thin line of trees.

They felt and heard the fire from the ME109 that was now closing in on their tail. Unable to outmanoeuvre the enemy with the stricken Mosquito, Eddie tried a dive as machine gun bullets tore through the airframe.

Charlie looked across and watched the flames start to flicker around the nacelle. Meanwhile, the Messerschmitt wheeled around for another run. The flames grew bigger, and smoke billowed from the cowling as the engine stuttered to a stop. Tracer fire raked through the wing, and the plane lost height.

Charlie took the aircraft down in a glide. They peered through the cockpit glass as they looked at the field, hoping it would make a suitable landing spot.

"Can you make that field, Flight?"

"Just about, Charlie. Hold on to your hat. This will be rough."

They braced as the aircraft belly-flopped into the field. The Mosquito hit hard. The world turned to noise—screeching metal, snapping wood, the violent crunch of impact. Its momentum took it for several hundred feet, ploughing up the mud before it came to a stop. Then stillness.

"Right, bail, now!" Charlie ordered, "before she blows."

Eddie needed no second telling. He slid the canopy back and clambered out of the cockpit into the wing. They scrambled away from the wreckage, boots crunching against hard, sun-baked earth. The air smelled of oil and fire. Smoke curled from the broken aircraft, the wreckage eerily quiet.

They ran as the aircraft exploded with a loud 'whump!' The scorching air pushed them down into the hard soil as debris was thrown up into the air and rained down around them.

They looked up, but the ME109 had gone, the pilot no doubt radioing back the news of his kill.

Charlie coughed. Blood trickled down his temple. "You alive?"

Eddie groaned, unclipping his harness. "More or less."

"Now what?" Charlie said.

"Find somewhere to hide first," Eddie said. There will be Jerries crawling all over this place before too long."

They started walking. Once on the road, they headed west towards the coast and Le Havre, their boots sounding loud on the tarmac. Charlie looked up at the sky.

"It's getting light. We need somewhere to hole up until tonight."

"We passed a farm just back there."

"Yes, let's go back. See if we can hide out in one of the outbuildings."

"What about rations?"

Charlie sighed. "We might be able to steal something from the farmyard if necessary."

They made their way to the farm. No one was about, so they climbed the gate and headed to the barn.

Inside, there were piles of hay, tools, and a tractor. They clambered up onto the pile of hay but stopped.

"*Arrêt!*"

They turned to look at the farmer, who held a shotgun at his hip. The man nodded to the ground, and the two airmen clambered back down. The farmer gestured at them to raise their hands. They complied. The farmer turned to the door. "*Ici!*"

The door opened a little more, and a woman came in. They looked at her. Her dark hair was partially concealed by a black beret, and she wore dark-colored clothing. At her hip, she held a Sten submachine gun. She smiled at the two airmen.

"Welcome to France, gentlemen. I am Flamme. You will come with me."

"Flamme?" Charlie said.

The woman inclined her head and smiled slightly. "That is all you need to know about me. It is better that way for all of us."

The two airmen looked at each other. "We have no choice, Flight," Charlie said.

Chapter 1

Lodève, Present Day

Patrice Laurent parked his car in the main car park in the shadow of the cathedral. The sun was getting up and the air was already warm as he and Pascale Hervé alighted and walked along Rue General Leclerc, bustling now with shoppers and tourists alike, to the bottom of the town before turning right, heading into the Arab quarter.

It seemed odd, Pascale thought, that everything was so familiar, yet so different. The new ring on her finger changed everything. Five years of widowhood were now officially over. She looked across at Patrice as he walked alongside her and caught his eye. He smiled and reached for her hand, grasping it gently as they walked. She noted the way the smile lit up his face. The spring air seemed sweet and fresh, and she breathed deeply. A new day, a new marriage, a new life.

For years, they had been colleagues who had worked together, learned to trust and know each other implicitly. The marriage was the final, logical conclusion. Now, for the first time in a long time, she felt contentment.

As usual, the office was in shadow, and the landlord had not fixed the light. They climbed the stairs to the first floor. Clarice and Radfield were already there, and as Pascale hung her coat on the rack, she noticed a man waiting in the inner office. She raised an eyebrow at Clarice.

"Did you have a good trip?" Clarice asked, ignoring the silent question.

"Thank you, yes," Pascale said. "We have a visitor?"

Clarice smiled. "Yes, he was in touch while you were away. He insisted upon seeing you in person as soon as you arrived back."

"What is it about?"

Clarice shrugged. "He didn't say much, but it was something to do with your grandmother."

Pascale frowned. "*Grand-mère*? What about her?"

"Ask, and you'll find out."

"*Fais pas ta maligne*," Pascale said, frowning at Clarice's smile and ignoring Patrice's broad grin. She took the proffered coffee and walked with Patrice into the inner office. The man stood and held out a hand in greeting.

The office was dimly lit, so Pascale placed her coffee on the desk and went to the blind to open it and let the sunlight into the room. "That's better," she said.

She looked around the room that Radfield and Clarice had been using while she and Patrice were away on their honeymoon. The desk was strewn with scattered case notes and a half-empty mug of cold coffee.

"Don't you two ever tidy up behind yourselves?" she said through the door to Clarice, who waved a hand dismissively.

"Too busy, madame."

"Pah!"

Pascale sat, pushing the files aside and turned her attention to the man who sat opposite, while Patrice sat next to her, sipping his coffee.

"Good morning, madame. I am Lucien Defrense," he said

Pascale looked at the man. *Late eighties*, she thought. He had a stiff bearing, so he possibly had a military background. The silvery hair was cropped short, and his eyeglasses had rubbed marks on the side of his head. His face was weathered, with dark circles under his eyes. He wore an old overcoat, but it was clean, and his suit was well-pressed. This was a man who was not well off but took pride in his appearance, but not his health, going by the blue tinge on his lips.

"What can I do for you, monsieur?" she said.

Defrense smiled. "I have been doing some research into my family history. My uncle was involved in the resistance during the war. As was my father, but he is not the one I am researching."

"Why is that?"

"Henri, my father, was executed by the SS. I know exactly what happened to him. It is my uncle who is the mystery."

Pascale watched him as she sipped her coffee. She was curious about the man but said nothing, preferring to let him speak uninterrupted. She would ask questions when he had finished his story.

Lucien seemed hesitant at first as he considered what he would say. She watched as he collected his thoughts, fiddling with the coffee cup in front of him. He seemed nervous, so she sat and let him speak when he had composed himself.

"Well, madame, that research leads me to you. More specifically, your maternal grandmother…" Lucien started but paused, leaving the words hanging in the air. He looked at Pascale, his gaze piercing but filled with something almost like regret. "What do you know of her, madam?"

"Claire Lemoine? Not much. Why?"

"Not much? So something, then. What little you do know would help, madame. Please, it is very important."

Pascale frowned and took another sip of her coffee. "That's the thing, I know very little. My mother told me nothing of note. She worked as a teacher in England at the beginning of the war. She met and married a member of De Gaulle's Free French shortly after the fall of France. He died in the fighting in Italy in 1943, leaving her with a small child—my mother."

"And then?"

Pascale shifted. "She disappeared. Her daughter, my mother, was raised by friends in England until after the war, when she went back to France to live with an aunt. That is all. No one knows what happened to Claire or why she disappeared. No one speaks of it. She vanished from the school where she was teaching. We wondered if she was killed in a bombing raid." She shrugged. "It was a long time ago. Before I was born, so I've never given it much thought."

"Weren't you curious?"

"Maybe, a little." She realised that she was the one being questioned here, but let it go. She could learn as much as she needed from answering his questions as from asking her own.

Lucien nodded. "Her name wasn't just Claire Lemoine. She was known as 'Flamme.' She was a resistance agent during the war."

Pascale froze, her expression unreadable for a moment.

D'accord. Now you've caught me off guard, monsieur.

Then slowly, the realisation dawned on her. Her grandmother, Claire Lemoine, the woman who vanished without a trace, had been a resistance agent. She had been in France all along.

"So, she didn't die in an air raid..."

"No."

"*D'accord*, it makes sense, I suppose. The disappearance. She vanished in England and reappeared over here."

Lucien continued, as he talked about the stories of Flamme's exploits. He talked of how she had helped smuggle vital information, sabotaged Nazi operations, and evaded capture time and time again, all while maintaining the appearance of an unassuming civilian.

"Where did you get this information?"

"It is on record. I have been delving into the archives."

The details left Pascale reeling. She had known so little of the woman and had never bothered to ask questions herself. She had merely accepted the family story of disappearing in England. This was something else entirely. She rubbed her temples as she took stock.

"She helped allied airmen get to Spain," Lucien said. "It was on an escape run to the Pyrenees that she and Jean-Luc vanished." He shrugged. "No one knows what happened. I can find no further information in the records after that. Which was why I thought that you might help."

Pascale could hear the bustle of traffic and voices in the street outside against the stillness of the office as she thought about the information. Eventually, she spoke.

"Why are you telling me this now?" she said. Her eyes narrowed as she studied Lucien, trying to decipher his intentions.

Lucien looked at her, his face a mixture of guilt and urgency. "Before I answer that, please look at this."

He pushed a faded photograph across the table. Pascale picked it up and peered at it before looking up at him. "Where did you get this?"

"That is Claire Lemoine, is it not?"

"Yes. I repeat, where did this come from?"

"The archives in Paris. This, madame, is la Flamme, a resistance operative who worked with a cell in the Rouen area from 1941 or 1942 to sometime in 1944, when all trace of them vanished."

"What do you want from me? I cannot tell you more than I already have."

Defrense looked around him. "This is a detective agency, madame. You know better than I how to uncover things that are lost. When I found the connection, I thought you might be intrigued enough to help me find the truth. What happened to Flamme and her unit?"

"And you? What are you hoping to achieve?"

Defrense reached for the photograph and pointed to another member of the group of young people. "See, there, that man?"

She nodded. A young man stared out at the faded image. Dark eyes looked through the mists of time into her own eyes.

"Jean Luc Dufresne, my uncle. Also known as Mirage. I want to know what happened to him. That is why now, and that is why I am asking you for help. We both have missing relatives, so maybe you can assist me in finding out what happened."

***

After Defrense left, the team gathered around the table. The others waited curiously for Pascale to divulge the outcome of her meeting with Defrense. She sat at the head of the room, processing the information he had just given her. She fiddled with her coffee cup, looking at it as if it held answers to the questions spinning around in her head. Her brow furrowed as she reflected on the revelation about her grandmother, Flamme, and her past as a resistance agent. She related her discussion with Defrense.

"Well, that was a revelation. I had no idea," she said. "I knew *grand-mère* was a teacher in England at the beginning of the war…"

"Teaching what?" Patrice said.

"French and German, to secondary age students."

"Ideal for recruitment, then," Patrice said.

***

Clarice leaned against the wall with her arms crossed, watching Pascale for any sign of emotional turmoil she might be feeling. She smiled; this one was coming her way. Clarice knew how to navigate the digital world, tracing pieces of information that no one else would catch. As the detective agency developed, they specialised in cold cases that the police were no longer interested in. But this time, there was a personal angle. This involved Pascale's personal history.

"I don't understand," Clarice broke the silence. "Your grandmother… Flamme, as Lucien called her. She disappeared, yes? No one ever really knew what happened to her." Her gaze shifted between Pascale and the rest of the team as if searching for clues in their faces. "But you said she disappeared before that, in England. So, she disappeared twice?"

***

Pascale nodded slowly, her thoughts drifting back to what her mother had said about Claire vanishing. "She went missing when my mother was young. One day, without warning. No trace. There was no body. It is all shrouded in the past, but she said nothing about any police investigation or anything like that. I suppose people went missing during bombing raids, and they assumed that was an explanation. Maybe. I don't know. They chalked it up to, well, a disappearance as if it were nothing. There was a war on, and people disappeared. But I always wondered if there was more, I suppose. Perhaps Defrense is right. Now is the time to find out and lay some ghosts to rest."

Radfield shifted in his chair and removed his glasses to polish them, as he was inclined to do when pondering a problem. He leaned forward and replaced his glasses, which made him look somewhat owl-like. He met Pascale's gaze as he spoke.

"People don't just vanish like that, not without someone or something involved," he said. "If she were killed in an air raid, there would be something on record. They didn't just dispose of bodies that were found in the wreckage. They tried to find out who they were. They had temporary morgues. They tagged bodies that they identified from documents in wallets and bags. If they did have unidentified bodies, they would have been photographed, and notes made. No, I don't believe that angle, frankly.

"Your mother might not have been aware, but there will be something. If SOE had recruited her, they would have managed that disappearance, so again, there will be something, somewhere, on record. If she was involved in the resistance, she was part of something dangerous. And the people who wanted her gone wouldn't just let it slide. They probably knew how to cover their tracks." He paused and looked at her as he weighed up the possibilities of what could have happened to Flamme.

"I think we should be looking at what happened first. Where was she, and what was she doing when she vanished in the UK? Look for the schoolteacher in England. That's what you said she was doing. The way I see this, there are two lines of investigation. One is the story known to your mother. What happened when Claire was in England? The second is the story that Monsieur Defrense told us about her exploits in France and subsequent disappearance in the Pyrenees. Are we talking about the same person? The photograph notwithstanding. Even back then, images could be faked. We need to look more closely at the provenance of that picture. I have some ideas about the first question, and I think it might be best if I went back to England to do a little digging."

Pascale exhaled heavily. "Good idea, David. You think she was involved with SOE? You believe Defrense's story?"

"That's exactly what I think. Your grandmother was a linguist, you said, so precisely the type of person they would recruit. French and German would have been too good a temptation. I need to speak to people who will let me look at the records."

Patrice reached out and smiled, placing a hand on Pascale's. She had come to rely on him in the past few years since Guillaume's death. He understood her better than anyone now, having helped her through the dark depression she experienced and the days he spent alongside her when she was in a coma following her attempted suicide. He remained calm, but his mind was clearly processing the same questions that swirled in Pascale's thoughts.

"You know, *Chérie*," Patrice said, "the past resurfaces when you least expect it. Maybe Lucien Defrense is telling the truth about Claire. Maybe she was more than just the mystery you never knew. If she was really part of something as important as the resistance, it's worth finding out. I say we do this."

Pascale looked at him, her lips pressed together as she listened. "It makes sense. But I cannot believe she would have left my mother like that, but she did, it seems. There's a contradiction. There has to be more to her disappearance." She stood up and walked about the room as she thought aloud.

"Right," Clarice said, her tone shifting into professional mode, her voice taking on that familiar, analytical edge that Patrice and Pascale had noted her taking since she had graduated from the *Université de Nîmes*. Almost, Pascale thought, as if she felt that her qualification as a detective gave her a newfound confidence in her abilities. Bossy, almost. Pascale made a mental note to nip it before it got out of hand, but that could wait.

"We're going to need to look deeper. I can dig through old government files and wartime records and see if there are any clues hidden in the digital archives. It's a start. Someone might need to go to Paris to look at physical records."

Radfield drummed his fingers on the desk. He sighed. "You're assuming they left clues. What if they went to great lengths to erase everything? They'd have been thorough, wouldn't they?"

"That's the problem," Patrice said. "The more thorough they are, the harder it will be to find any trace of her."

"Then we'll just have to dig harder. If she was part of something that important, someone would know something, and we'll find it," Pascale said.

The team fell silent for a moment, each thinking about what they had just heard. They could hear the sounds of vehicles and voices drifting up from outside. The sun shone through the open blinds and filled the room with light, illuminating motes of dust floating in the air that hung heavy with the odour of coffee. Each of them was lost in the thoughts whirring in their minds. It felt like a clock had started ticking again for Pascale and her grandmother's legacy.

Clarice broke the silence, her voice again taking on that analytical tone. "I'll start by looking into the old resistance networks, cryptic messages, encrypted files, or survivors from that time. If your grandmother was really Flamme, there may be hidden records that can point us in the right direction."

Pascale nodded. "Do it. I want to know what happened to her, to *us*. It's time to bring this out into the light, no matter what."

Radfield removed his glasses again and began polishing them despite having already done so. "We'll find what's hidden, Pascale. The truth has a habit of surfacing. We just have to look."

"If we start digging into the past, there is the possibility that we uncover things that some might want to remain hidden," Patrice said.

"That thought went through my mind," Radfield said. "And should that happen, we'll be ready for whoever tries to stop us. In the meantime, I'll book a ticket from Béziers. I'll make a start with the National Archives at Kew. Leave the UK end to me."

"You might want to speak to Maman," Clarice said.

Radfield smiled. Since arriving in France, his relationship with Laurence, Clarice's mother, had blossomed, and he was now a fixture in their old house in Pégairolles. "I'll talk to her this evening," he said.

The team looked at each other. They had made their decision. Their focus shifted from their individual roles to the shared mission. This was no longer just about solving a case. It was about uncovering the secrets buried deep in the past and ensuring Flamme's legacy and Pascale's place within it would never be buried again.

Pascale sat drinking her coffee and looking at the photograph for a while. Clarice went back to her computer, and the sound of the keyboard rattling carried through from her office. They could hear Radfield booking a flight. Pascale wondered if he planned to take Laurence with him. She would enjoy visiting England while he was digging around in the past.

"How many tickets are you booking, David?" she called out.

Radfield grinned. "You think I should take Laurence?"

Clarice looked up from her screen. "If you don't, you will never be forgiven."

"Got it," he said.

Patrice sat down and looked at the photographs.

"So," he said, "you didn't know any of this?"

Pascale shook her head. "No. *Grand-mère* just vanished with no explanation. It was a family mystery. Now I find that she vanished twice. Once is unfortunate, twice is carelessness…"

He smiled. "Now that mystery deepens, eh?"

"Yes, and now I have to find out what really happened to her. I need to go and see my mother."

Chapter 2

England, October 1941

The late evening sky was growing dark with thick cloud cover, ideal for a clandestine drop. The damp air was sharp with the scent of wet earth, and fine water droplets clung to the coats of the two men waiting by the airstrip. Arthur Spencer stood on the tarmac, his coat collar turned up against the chill, scanning the horizon as the Westland Lysander's engine sputtered to life. The engine's noise was deafening, a constant drone that cut through the quiet of the airfield.

Beside him, Vanguard stood with a stoic composure, his eyes fixed on the aircraft. To Spencer, as he held his hat in place while the backdraft threatened to sweep it away, he seemed very young. Tall and youthful. It occurred to Spencer that this young man was almost young enough to be his son. A pang of guilt crossed his soul. Too young, he felt. He wondered if they would meet again or if he was sending another agent to his death. They said nothing. There was no need. Vanguard was a man of few words, even fewer now that the mission was underway. They both knew what was at stake.

The Lysander was ready. The ground crew were already making last-minute adjustments, their movements swift and efficient, as much a machine as the aircraft they were prepping. There was no room for error on a mission like this. The aircraft's engine roared, spitting flames from the exhausts, and Vanguard glanced at Spencer, his expression unreadable.

"You know the plan?" Spencer's voice cut through the noise. "Blend in and do nothing until you are activated."

Vanguard nodded once. No need for reassurance. He had been trained. He was ready. Now, there was no turning back. He was about to fly into occupied Europe, where danger lurked at every turn, and the slightest slip could lead to betrayal and death.

The aircraft turned, ready for take-off. Vanguard didn't flinch. His gaze remained fixed on the plane as it turned and paused while the pilot awaited orders.

"Take care," Spencer said, his voice barely audible above the engine noise. He slapped his agent on the back, watched as he walked across the tarmac, and clambered into the rear cockpit. He raised a hand before sliding the canopy shut and looked ahead.

The Lysander's engine note increased as it moved forward, accelerating down the runway and lifting off the ground with a smooth, deliberate motion. Arthur Spencer had already turned his back on it, the plane climbing steadily into the low clouds, merging with the dark sky, its engine note diminishing as it ascended into the eastern sky. It would be over Germany in a couple of hours. Spencer briefly looked back, watched it for a moment longer, then turned on his heel and moved swiftly to his car, where his driver sat patiently waiting.

He could feel the pressure building, that unshakable sense that the next few hours would make or break everything. Vanguard was now in the air, and once he touched down behind enemy lines, there would be no turning back. There would be no way of knowing what kind of reception he would receive, nor any way of knowing if this would be the last time Spencer saw him.

But there was no time for doubt; the mission was in motion, and Spencer, as always, would follow it wherever it led.

***

England, November 1941

As Claire Lemoine packed her desk at the small school in Leatherhead, the sound of excited conversations in the hallway gradually faded as the day's final bell rang. Outside, children called out and played, filling the air with their laughter. Inside, the early winter sunlight streamed through the crisscross of tape on the windows, casting strange shadows across the desks. A calm settled in after the busy day. The school, nestled in Leatherhead, just a stone's throw from Oxshott Woods, served as a refuge not only for the children who came to learn but also for Claire, who, though displaced from her homeland, was finding an opportunity to rebuild her life. She thought about her husband, Gérard, who was away in Africa. All she could tell herself was that no news was good news, even though she worried about the day when the telegram would arrive to bring bad news.

She neatly stacked the books on her desk, carefully brushing the dust off the covers of textbooks in French, Italian, and German. There was a faint odour of chalk in the air. The voices receded, leaving the room silent as she busied herself with preparing the room for the following day.

Despite the war that raged across Europe, Claire's days in Leatherhead were simple. She taught languages to eager students, sharing her culture and offering them a glimpse of a world that was now a distant memory.

She looked around the room and sighed. As she reached for her coat and bag, she heard a door creak open somewhere in the hallway outside. Frowning, she turned to see a tall, sharp-featured man standing in the doorway, exuding an air of quiet authority. His appearance was polished, with a dark, well-pressed suit and a fedora hat partially shielding his eyes.

"Excuse me, Madame Lemoine?" he said, lifting the hat slightly so that she could see clear blue eyes that looked at her with a quiet intensity.

"Yes," she said. "How may I help you?"

He smiled, but she sensed something shrouded in his demeanour that lay beneath the outward geniality.

"Arthur Spencer. I wonder if I could have a little of your time, madame."

Claire paused and looked at him. He held himself erect with a military bearing despite wearing civilian clothing. She watched as he pushed back his fedora, reached into his coat pocket, pulled out a cigarette case, and placed one on his lips. He held the case out to her, but she declined. He lit a match and drew on the tobacco as it caught the flame. She remained silent through the little ritual, her hand resting on the edge of her desk, watching him, wondering what he was here for. She supposed that he would state his case eventually, and she was content to wait.

She had no idea who this man was, but his expression suggested he wasn't there for small talk. She met his gaze, her instincts sharpening, a feeling of unease settling in her stomach.

"I have nowhere special to go, Monsieur, so we can walk together if you like. I will listen to whatever you have to say. There is nothing bad about Gérard, I hope," she said cautiously.

Arthur shook his head and stepped in line alongside her as they walked along the corridor past the classrooms. "No," he said. "It has nothing to do with your husband," he said, shifting his tone slightly. "I'm with a special office of the British government. The war is escalating, and we need people with your unique skills. The kind that can make a difference."

Claire furrowed her brow as she pushed open the door, stepping into the chilly sunshine. He walked alongside her across the playground to the gates and the road outside. It felt so peaceful, almost as if there were no war. The air was cool, and summer was a fading memory, taking with it the golden leaves on the trees of the Oxshott woods. Above, she heard an engine and looked up.

"Spitfire," he said, bringing the reality of war sharply into focus.

She looked across at the man. His hat shaded his face, and he walked like a soldier, cementing her original thought that this was a military man. He drew on his cigarette as he walked, eventually flicking the stub into the air to land on the pavement, where he ground it under his heel.

"I'm not sure I understand," Claire said, her voice steady but tinged with scepticism. "I am a schoolteacher. I am not involved in any government affairs."

Arthur's lips curled into a faint smile, though without humour. "You speak four languages fluently. French, Italian, German, and English. I wonder if your German is as accented as your English? I can detect a very slight accent, but it is faint. A native speaker would detect that you are foreign, but only just."

"Mein Deutsch ist genauso gut wie mein Englisch."

He nodded. "Very good. They said you were fluent."

"You speak it as well?"

"Yes, madame. I am fluent in German and spent some of my youth in Germany. I feel you would pass as German from somewhere close to the French border, should that be necessary. Alsace, perhaps. Your language skills are invaluable in the kind of work we do. We need people who can move in and out of enemy territories, blend in seamlessly, and gather information. And, if necessary, fight."

Claire felt a chill run down her spine. "I have never fought. I am not a soldier. I wouldn't know how."

"Madame, many of our operatives have never fought. That is why we exist. To train people to prepare to go into occupied Europe and engage the enemy. We need people who will blend in. Your language skills are precisely what we seek."

The thought of espionage, of returning to France to fight a clandestine war, was daunting. Yet, as much as she tried to ignore it, the idea of resistance stirred something within her. She had lost so much already—her family, her home in France—all swallowed up by the horrors of the war. Maybe it was time to do more than wait and teach. If Gérard was out fighting the Boche in Africa, she could play her part. However, there was a problem.

She looked at him as she pulled her books closer to her body. "And what would this involve, exactly?"

"We will train you and then send you back to France. It will be somewhat more dangerous than teaching languages. It will involve sabotage, intelligence gathering, and, if necessary, working undercover in hostile territories. I already have an agent in the field. I need someone who can support him, serving as a conduit between him and me. You would be part of a network aimed at weakening the enemy's grip and keeping them tied down and distracted. Make the occupation as difficult as possible while we gather our forces to strike back. Then there are the escape lines. We want to get back any allied aircrews as we are short enough as it is. The local partisan groups are doing an excellent job with that, but someone from our organisation on the ground, coordinating activities, will strengthen the effort. We've already seen how effective someone like you can be."

"What about my daughter Colette? She needs me."

Spencer smiled. "Have no fear on that score. We can make the necessary arrangements for her care, regardless of what may happen."

That 'regardless of what may happen, sent a chill down her spine. That would always be there, lurking, waiting, the cost of it all going wrong.

"The 'what may happen' is something to consider," she said aloud.

"I cannot sugarcoat it, madame. The Nazis are ruthless with any spies they capture. You can expect to be tortured and executed." He paused and added a warning. "The life of a field operative is dangerous and short. Be under no illusion on that score."

She tightened her lips. "Thank you for being so frank."

"There is no point in you not understanding what you will be letting yourself in for. But we must win this war, and we need people like you on the ground in occupied Europe to do it."

Claire remained silent for a moment, contemplating the gravity of his words. She stopped by a gate set in a wall leading up to a small, terraced house. "This is where I live, Monsieur."

"I know."

"You seem to know a lot."

"It's my job."

Spencer looked at her, his eyes hard as he met her gaze. "I understand this is a lot to consider. But we're in a time when our choices can help to change the course of history."

She closed her eyes briefly, her thoughts rushing through her mind like a storm. She could remain in her small, safe world, teaching languages and living with the memory of what she had lost. Alternatively, she could take a different path that would demand every ounce of courage she had left.

Claire finally looked at Spencer and nodded. "I will think about it, Monsieur. I cannot promise more than that at the moment. I have a great deal to think about. Not least Colette."

He gave a slight nod, his expression unreadable. "I expect nothing less, madame. I'll be in touch. And Claire, this might be the most important choice you will ever make."

"It could also be the most fatal."

He inclined his head, conceding the point.

As he turned to leave, Claire felt the weight of his words settling on her shoulders. She glanced down at the pile of exercise books in her arms, which she would be marking that evening. She had been teaching others to learn the language of their enemy. Now, it seemed, it was her turn to learn a new language: that of war.

***

Rouen, 1941

The damp air of northern France greeted Heinrich Vogel as his train arrived at Rouen Rue Verte. The smell of steam filled his lungs, and the clanking and hissing of the locomotive and the tannoy calling out platforms, along with the chatter of people on the platforms, filled his ears as he stepped onto the platform. He walked through the concourse and out into the cool morning drizzle and shivered as the cold damp air hit him. The city was cloaked in a dreary grey cloud, and he looked up at it briefly before turning his eyes to the streets around him. The gothic architecture juxtaposed with the glaring presence of Nazi occupation. The red, white, and black flags of the Reich hung from several buildings nearby, a stark reminder of his purpose here. He breathed deeply and held himself straight as he looked about him for his driver.

In his late twenties, he was still young but had quickly risen through the party after joining the SS. His uniform felt heavy with responsibility and power. Its black fabric served as a shield and a symbol of authority, while the death's head insignia on his cap instilled fear in those who saw him approaching. As an SS-Untersturmführer, he was there to enforce the will of the Reich, to root out any hint of defiance, no matter how small. His orders were clear: eliminate the resistance, punish the families who dared harbour insurgents, and maintain order by any means necessary.

He straightened his cap, brushed a few stray strands of dark hair from his forehead, and scanned the station for his contact. The air was colder than he expected, but he wasn't about to let it distract him. He was selected for this post due to his efficiency, ruthlessness, and belief that his steady hand could handle whatever resistance cells had taken root in this city. Like much of occupied France, Rouen would fall under his control, and soon, all of Normandy would know that the Reich's will was unbreakable.

A tall, thin sergeant approached him, a briefcase in hand and a cigarette dangling from his lips. The man saluted sharply.

"Untersturmführer Vogel," the sergeant said, his voice cold and professional. "Welcome to Rouen. I am Werner Schäfer. I trust your journey was uneventful?"

"It was, Unterscharführer," Vogel said. "Is everything prepared for my arrival?"

"Of course, Untersturmführer. We've been expecting you," Schäfer said, dropping the remains of his cigarette and grinding it into the ground. He gestured toward an open-top black Mercedes parked at the side of the station. "I'll drive you to your quarters, and then you'll report to the Sicherheitsdienst headquarters. Obersturmführer Richter is expecting you."

Vogel nodded, disregarding small talk. His gaze swept over the city as the two men approached the car, barely noticing the man by the ticket booth, extinguishing his cigarette. The streets felt unnaturally quiet, as if the people were holding their breath, anticipating something. He could already sense the tension in the air. The resistance, although subtle, was palpable. He had been briefed on the underground network in the area. The French would resist, but he intended to demonstrate the futility of their defiance. His job wasn't merely to subdue the people; it was to crush the spirit of rebellion, to make an example of anyone who dared to challenge the Reich.

Schäfer drove swiftly through the narrow streets, passing groups of soldiers and civilians. While some local traffic delivered supplies, others walked or cycled. Most of the vehicles on the roads were German military or SS officers in their black Mercedes staff cars, like him. The locals kept their heads lowered, avoiding eye contact. Every corner and every shadow seemed to conceal a secret. Somewhere in the city, an undercurrent of defiance grew stronger beneath the surface, which he could sense. The French peasants loathed him and everything he represented, and he revelled in the power it provided over them as he sat in the back of the car, smoking a cigarette and surveying his new dominion. A thrill coursed through his veins as that sense of power enveloped him. He was the hand of justice, the force that would bring this city to heel. Resistance would be met with swift retribution.

Having dropped his bags off at his designated apartment, they drove to the headquarters of the local SD. Schäfer stopped before the building, and Vogel flicked the cigarette stub out as he stood. He stepped out, his boots clicking sharply against the stone steps. As he ascended, he couldn't help but feel that this moment, this city, would mark the beginning of something much greater. His ascent in the SS had only just begun, and Rouen was merely the start of his mission to cleanse France of the insurgents threatening the Reich.

Inside the SD headquarters, the atmosphere was thick with tension. The officers there greeted him with a mix of respect and wariness. They understood the significance of his arrival—he would be the one to root out the resistance in the region. His reputation for efficiency and brutal determination had preceded him.

A man in his mid-forties with the insignia of an Obersturmführer on his uniform motioned for Vogel to follow him into a back office. The room was sparse. A heavy desk dominated the centre, flanked by maps of the area and dossiers of suspected resistance members.

"Untersturmführer Vogel," the officer held out a hand. "I am Franz Richter. You will be reporting directly to me." His voice was gravelly and serious. "You've been given a critical task. The resistance here has become more organised and daring. We need someone who can deal with them swiftly. This morning, several Wehrmacht soldiers were murdered in a raid on a troop column outside the city. I need to send a message."

Vogel nodded. "Round up some civilians?"

Richter smiled. "I like your thinking, Untersturmführer. However, that is a task we can leave for our colleagues in the Gestapo. I have another idea."

Vogel raised an eyebrow.

"Yes, but first, take this and digest it." Richter handed him a thick file. "This is your mission. Find the cells. Exterminate them. Leave nothing behind. We cannot afford to let these rats multiply."

"If we are not to round up people, then what do you have in mind?"

Richter smiled. "Some counterintelligence, Untersturmführer. A man on the inside, and you will run him."

Vogel's fingers tightened around the file, the paper creaking under his grip. He had been trained for this and for what he had joined the SS to do. This was his moment.

"Understood," Vogel said, saluting, his voice cold, as his eyes scanned the documents before him. The resistance would not stand a chance. They would be silenced swiftly and without mercy.

***

As Vogel met Schäfer at the station, they were being watched. Leaning indolently against a wall at the end of the concourse, his coat collar pulled up against the chill, Jean-Luc Defrense appeared to anyone who might notice to be absorbed in his cigarette and waiting for a train, oblivious to the outside world. He had been there for hours, watching the trains come and go, blending in with the crowd of civilians. However, his eyes were not on the commuters but on the officers and soldiers. Specifically, he was waiting for the arrival of one man, Untersturmführer Vogel. Word had reached him that Vogel was coming. Recent sabotage attacks on German supply lines and the rail infrastructure were bound to provoke a reaction eventually. Untersturmführer Vogel was no ordinary Nazi. He was apparently one of Himmler's own. A rising star, and stories of his casual cruelty preceded him.

Jean-Luc's attention shifted as the approaching train slowed. The metal wheels screeched against the rails as the brakes brought the train to a halt, followed by the hiss of steam as the driver released the pressure. He watched the soldiers disembark, their boots clicking against the platform. Their faces were unfamiliar and cold. Then, a figure emerged from the carriage wearing a crisp black SS uniform, his posture rigid and his face set in an arrogant half-smile. Jean-Luc tensed.

So, this is him. Vogel.

He was tall, younger than Jean-Luc had expected, perhaps in his mid-20s, but something was chilling about how he carried himself. Even among the hardened officers, he seemed to command attention. His cap, adorned with the death's head insignia of the SS, sat at a sharp, precise angle, giving it a slightly jaunty look that contrasted with everything it represented. Every movement was deliberate and efficient.

Vogel stepped down from the train, adjusting his uniform as if already preparing for the task ahead. He didn't seem out of place here; the station bustled with activity as soldiers, locals, and officers moved in a steady rhythm. Yet, there was a coldness about him, an air of superiority that seemed to separate him from the crowd. Vogel was no ordinary officer—Jean-Luc could feel it in the way he looked at the city and how his eyes scanned the surroundings like a predator, searching for something.

Once Vogel set foot on the platform, a sergeant approached him and began to speak. Vogel nodded without hesitation, and the man gestured toward a black car parked at the front of the station. Jean-Luc watched closely, his eyes narrowing as the men made their way toward the car, passing so close that he could almost touch them. The thought flitted across his mind that he could just pull out his pistol and kill the man here and now, doing everyone a favour even if he died in the act. However, this thought never materialised beyond wishful thinking, and he watched as they walked past, unaware of his presence.

Jean Luc pinched his cigarette and let the stub fall to the ground, never taking his eyes off Vogel as he walked with the sergeant to an open-top Mercedes staff car.

Jean Luc followed from a distance and stepped out onto the road outside, where the two Germans were getting into the car. He had seen enough of the SS and their cruelty. Rouen had suffered under their boots since the fall of France, and now it seemed the city would face even darker times with the arrival of this young man. Jean-Luc had heard the whispers that Vogel was sent here for a reason. A ruthless reason.

The car's engine sputtered to life, and Vogel was taken away, disappearing into the light mist, leaving only the lingering tension in his wake.

Jean Luc looked across the street and nodded to André Fournier, who was waiting by his bicycle. Fournier mounted the machine and pedalled away.

***

Café Lys Noir, Rouen, Autumn, 1941

Suzanne Moreau was an attractive young woman approaching thirty. This evening, she was dressed to kill. Her long, dark hair was combed straight, forming curtains around her pale face. She wore a beret that she had perched jauntily on her head, a Breton shirt that clung to her figure, tight slacks and sandals and a small clutch bag. The ensemble was stylish, alluring, and disarming, albeit unusual. She wanted to attract attention, and that was what she got. A few disapproving stares from locals, whom she treated with a smile and some Gestapo officers looked but said nothing. Again, she smiled. They weren't her target. The image she presented was designed, like the nectar on the honeydew, to attract a particular prey.

She sat at a corner table near the door and watched from early evening, when it was quiet, to the busy period, when the clientele started filling the place with laughter, chatter, cigarette smoke, and the smell of coffee and brandy. She sat patiently, stringing out her glass of brandy, barely sipping it as the time passed, awaiting her prey. She looked across the room, where Marguerite and André Fournier were working the bar and keeping an eye on her. They would briefly catch her glance and then look away, preoccupied with their work.

A group of around a half dozen off-duty Wehrmacht soldiers came in. They were already flushed with drink, shouting and laughing, looking for a good night out. A few of them caught sight of Suzanne and gave appreciative whistles and comments. She smiled and said nothing. She waited.

Eventually, drawn by the bait, tall, blond, blue-eyed and heavily built, one, wearing the insignia of an Unteroffizier, came over and sat opposite her, landing heavily in the chair, his cigarette dangling from his mouth and a slightly glazed look in his eyes. He belched and hiccoughed.

"*Entschuldigung, Fräulein.* I think I may be drunk. Can I buy you a drink?" he said, looking pointedly at her empty glass.

"Merci," she said. "I'll have a cognac."

The man lifted an arm, "*Garçon, garçon,*" he said, snapping his fingers.

André smiled at her and came over.

"Monsieur?"

"Two brandies," the man said.

"Certainly."

André returned to the bar, spoke to Marguerite, who prepared the drinks, and walked across, placing them on the table.

"I'm Ernst," the soldier said, gulping back his drink. "Who are you, sweetheart?"

"Suzanne."

"Well, Suzanne. I am pleased to meet you." He hiccoughed again and looked down at his glass, which was now empty, and was about to order another when Marguerite placed another on the table, smiling briefly at Suzanne.

"You want another?" Ernst said, noticing that Suzanne hadn't touched her drink.

She shook her head. "I am good." She took a sip and watched as Ernst downed his, slamming the glass on the table with such force, she wondered if it would break.

This went on for several more drinks, with Marguerite seamlessly making sure that there was a full glass for Ernst before he had time to think about ordering another.

Now, seriously worse for the drink, he decided it was time to ask Suzanne to go somewhere less busy.

"I'd be delighted," she said, stifling the disgust reflex as she rose and reached out to help him to his feet. "Come on, let's get you up and outside."

Unnoticed by Ernst's colleagues, who were now singing drinking songs and pouring lagers down their throats, they slipped outside into the cool air of the deserted street. Ernst leaned heavily against Suzanne, and she silently cursed his weight. She supported him as they walked, stumbling through the darkening streets until she came to a quiet alleyway where she had placed her bicycle earlier in the evening.

"Here," she said.

She leaned back against the wall and stifled her desire to push him away as he fell against her, trying to put his tongue into her mouth as a hand fumbled with her slacks. Then he went limp. Behind him, André stood with his knife, wet with blood in his hands. Ernst was now a dead weight that pressed against her body, making it difficult to breathe.

"Get this lump off me, André," she said.

André pulled Ernst back and lowered him gently to the floor.

"Time we weren't here," he said. He looked down at the body. "They will find him tomorrow."

Suzanne sighed. "I hope we don't pay too heavy a price."

"It's war, André said. There will always be casualties in war."

"I know. I don't have to like it, though."

"You and me both," he said.

They went back to the alleyway's entrance, and having decided that it was clear, they went in opposite directions: André went back to the Café Lys Noir, and Suzanne mounted her bike and pedalled home at a leisurely pace as if nothing untoward had just happened.

***

Lodève, Present Day

Radfield was drowning under a mountain of dog. Two dogs, to be precise. Queenie and Melchett had taken a shine to him since his arrival in Pégairolles to live with Laurence Gunthier. He accepted that Laurence was a dog person and if he was going to love her, he would have to love her dogs.

Not that he minded the two border collies in a detached sort of way. It was just that whenever he sat on the sofa, they assumed he wanted both of them in his lap. And he wasn't entirely convinced that he did, besides which, there was more dog than there was lap, which created something of a strategic problem.

Fortunately, rescue was at hand.

"Down, the pair of you," Laurence said, with just the right level of scolding in her voice to encourage the animals to retreat to the floor. They sat there, watching, tongues lolling, waiting for their next opportunity to pounce. Laurence busied herself in the kitchen while Radfield looked up at her, taking in the dark Mediterranean looks and swift, precise movements. He often wondered how, after all the years of being single, he managed to get so lucky. She looked up and caught him watching and rewarded him with a smile.

"So, what are the plans?"

"We'll fly to London. I can do a little research at the archives. I don't know what I'll find, but I expect something will turn up."

"Clarice can look after those two," Laurence said, shooting the dogs a look. "Pascale won't mind if she takes them to the office. She's done it before."

"If you say so," Radfield replied, eyeing the dogs warily in case they decided a moment of weakness was about to open up. Their tails wagged in unison as the stand-off continued.

***

There was a quiet energy in the office the following morning as the team dispersed to their tasks. Radfield busied himself booking his travel and accommodation arrangements for the trip to London, while Clarice tapped away at her keyboard, searching for digital traces of Claire's past. Pascale lingered by the corkboard, her eyes tracing the faded photograph of her grandmother, Claire Lemoine, standing among the resistance fighters. Lucien Defrense's words played on her mind: She was known as Flamme. So, what happened to her? All she knew as a child was that Grand-mère had disappeared during the war. There was never a mention of her involvement in the resistance. Now that she knew about it, the mystery of Claire's life felt like a thread pulling her into the past, one she couldn't ignore.

Patrice joined her at the corkboard, pinning a copy of Defrense's notes next to the photograph. He glanced at her, his expression a mix of curiosity and concern. "What next?" he asked, surveying the scattered pieces of information.

Pascale turned to him, a glint in her eye. "A little motorcycle ride," she said, a faint smile playing on her lips, knowing he never understood her passion for riding, so enjoying herself. "I think I'll pay Maman a visit. I've not seen her since the wedding. It'll be nice to catch up."

Patrice raised an eyebrow, a teasing note in his voice. "And interrogate her about the past, eh?"

Pascale's smile widened into a playful grin. "Well, as you put it like that. I'll give her your love."

He laughed, the sound warm and familiar, easing the weight of the investigation for a moment. "You do that, Chérie."

She grabbed her jacket from the rack and headed for the door, the faint scent of coffee lingering in the air. As she stepped outside, Patrice heard the deep, throaty rumble of the big V-twin engine of her Indian FTR coming to life. He watched through the window as she pulled away, the bike's maroon livery catching the sunlight, carrying her toward Le Crès and toward answers about a past she'd never truly known. He shook his head. She was right, he would never understand her passion for two wheels. He looked across at Clarice, who smiled and shrugged.

* * *

Oxshott Heath, Late Autumn, 1941

Claire wheeled the heavy steel pushchair ahead of her. Colette gurgled quietly as they bumped over the uneven path. After a while, Claire stopped and spread a blanket on the ground, settling down with the child by her side, while above, she could hear the faint drone of engines.

Sunday afternoons were an oasis in the busy week—a calm before the storm of Monday morning routines, classroom noise, and evenings marking textbooks and setting the following day's lessons. Time seemed to slow down almost to a standstill here on the heath. She needed to think. To reflect.

Spencer's words had been swirling in her mind since his visit a few days ago. His proposal was laced with personal danger and sacrifice. With a child to consider and a husband somewhere at war, that proposal weighed heavily. If she went, she would be leaving Colette behind. Perhaps for good. Was that something she could justify? Was it selfless or selfish? She had a choice. Others didn't. She could stay. No one would be any the wiser. Except, of course, *she* would know. Whatever decision she made, her conscience would need to be clear.

And yet... others went to war *because* they had children. Gérard had made his decision as soon as France was invaded. Child or not, he would fight the Boche. He had relied on Claire to keep their daughter safe, and when France fell, she had done just that, getting out just before the Wehrmacht reached Paris.

Now, here in the pastoral shadow of the Oxshott woods, she could raise Colette and hope that Gérard would return once it was all over.

But how long would that be?

It had already been over a year since the fall of France and the Battle of Britain. The lull that followed offered a deceptive sense of peace. She looked up at the trees, their bare branches reaching out to the sky. Crows squabbled overhead, the last of the leaves drifting down to join the damp mulch underfoot. The air smelled of its decay, and the earth, mingled with the sharp freshness of the turning season.

What should she do? Go and fight and perhaps die? Or stay, safe, and raise her child? The droning above grew louder as the aircraft came closer, causing her to look up. She saw aircraft circling high above. They swooped and dived, twisting in tight formation. She heard the faint chatter of machine-gun fire. One plane trailed smoke as others surged after it in pursuit.

An elderly man passed by, walking his dog, glancing skyward.

"Is it one of ours?" she asked, shielding her eyes from the glare.

He shook his head. "No, miss. That's a Junkers 88. Reconnaissance plane. Ours are the ones chasing it—Hurricanes."

He walked on, calling to his dog. Claire kept watching the aerial battle, subconsciously holding her breath as the sky turned into a killing ground. So distant, like toys, yet so deadly for those involved.

Men were dying up there for their country. What was it Spencer said? "People with your language skills can help to turn the tide." She subconsciously held her breath as she watched the dogfight.

She looked down at Colette and sighed.

"Who will die for you, *ma chérie*, eh? And who will look after you if I go. And if I die, what future will you have?"

Chapter 3

Le Crès, near Montpellier, Present Day

Pascale rolled into the quiet, sun-dappled road on the outskirts of Le Crès. The Indian FTR burbled softly as she pulled up to the gravel driveway of her mother's house. The bike was sleek and powerful, featuring a distinctive maroon livery and a black lattice frame cradling the big V-twin engine. This American machine stood apart from its stablemates because it was not a cruiser. Styled after the company's successful flat track racers and equipped with small seventeen-inch wheels, it looked more European than American and handled with a quickness that cruisers lacked. Given its relatively short manufacturing run, owners of these machines now possessed a future classic, and Pascale was aware of it as she looked down at it and smiled.

The polished paintwork glinted under the late afternoon sun. The sound of the engine cut off. The stillness in the air was broken only by the ticking of the cooling engine and the cicadas chirping in the trees. The air was heavy with the heat of the afternoon swelter.

Colette Hervé's house was nestled against the backdrop of sprawling fields and a scattering of trees. It featured rustic stone walls and a fastidiously manicured garden where she would be seen most days, dead-heading, pruning or weeding. Woe betide any weed that dared to show its shoots in Colette Hervé's garden. The wind picked up slightly, causing the leaves of the olive trees to rustle. A reminder of the charm of the southern French countryside. The smell of lavender drifted by, and above, Pascale could see the contrails of an aircraft heading to or from Montpellier airport as they dissipated in the azure sky.

Pascale removed her helmet, her dark hair falling free as she surveyed the scene. The house felt timeless and comforting with its cosy, weathered exterior and small windows framed by a vine that clung to the stone as it crept up the walls. The faded shutters, now partly open, let in the golden light of the late afternoon, which cast a warm glow on the stone path leading to the front door.

She took a moment to appreciate the serenity of this place and memories of growing up here, and reflect on the reason for her visit before kicking the side stand into place and stepping off the bike. The soft crunch of gravel beneath her boots punctuated the stillness. She headed toward the door along the pathway, which was lined with pots of bright red geraniums. Bees busied themselves flitting from one plant to another, their hum gentle on the warm air. The light briefly framed her silhouette as she approached the house, ready for the familiar embrace of family. She stepped up to the front door and rang the bell. Inside, she could hear the chimes echoing through the house. After a few moments, Colette Hervé opened it. She smiled upon seeing her daughter and invited her in.

"Pascale, this is a nice surprise. What brings you here?"

"Can't I visit my mother?"

The older woman laughed. "There will be a reason. There is always a reason."

"*Eh, bien*, you know me too well, *Maman chérie*."

"Come on in, and I'll get a coffee. You can tell me about it."

Colette fussed over preparing coffee while Pascale sat, and they chatted about Pascale's honeymoon and the gossip concerning her colleagues, carefully avoiding the purpose of the visit.

"Patrice is good for you, Pascale. You have a glow about you these days."

When the coffee was on the table, Pascale and Colette sat across from each other at the old wooden table in the kitchen. The warm light from the window cast soft shadows across their faces. The room smelled faintly of rosemary and thyme, the herbs drying on the windowsill that would add flavour to a boeuf bourguignon. Outside, the faint sound of cicadas chirped in the background, but inside, it was just the quiet murmur of family history hanging in the air.

Still wearing the faint traces of the ride on her leather jacket, Pascale relaxed with her coffee, in no hurry to get to the point. She took a few moments to enjoy the memories of the place where she grew up and the quiet companionship of her mother. Colette was in her late eighties, with once-dark hair now turned iron-grey. She looked up from her coffee. She sensed that something heavy was weighing on Pascale's mind. She smiled. "Well, what brings you here, Pascale?"

"*Maman*," Pascale began, her voice a little unsteady as she thought about how to frame her thoughts, "We had a visit from a gentleman called Lucien Defrense the other day. He has been doing some research into his family history."

"And why did he come to you? For help with the research?"

"In part. But he didn't know what we did until he stumbled upon my name. He discovered something. About *Grand-mère* Lemoine." She paused, her fingers tracing the rim of her own cup. "She was a part of the French Resistance during the war."

Colette placed her cup down on the table, her expression unreadable. The brief silence between them felt charged, like the calm before a storm. She looked at Pascale and furrowed her brow.

"What do you mean? She was...?" Colette's voice trailed off as if she were unsure whether to believe the words or if they were even possible.

Pascale took a breath. "He found letters, old documents, even photographs. There are accounts of her working with the resistance. She was involved in some of the more covert operations, helping to smuggle allied airmen out of occupied France. But... there's something else. She went on a mission, and she vanished. There's no trace of what happened to her after the war ended."

Colette's face tightened. For a moment, she said nothing as she collected her thoughts. "I never knew anything about that. I barely remember her. I was an infant when she vanished in England, not France."

Pascale watched her mother closely, noticing the flicker of something. Perhaps sadness or a sense of lost time in her eyes. "Do you remember anything, *maman*? Any details? Anything that could help explain what happened? We will do the research, but if you have anything that could help, it would be a good place to start."

Colette leaned back in her chair, her coffee held mid-air, and her gaze lost in thought. "I remember stories," she said, reflecting on her distant childhood.

"Small things that never made sense then. I remember a man visiting when I was younger, but he was always in a hurry, always speaking in hushed tones. He came once or twice that summer, and then she was gone. I never saw either of them again. I didn't understand it then. But when I asked about it, people would change the subject. It was like there was a part of her life she couldn't talk about. But I never knew it was this."

"What happened to you? You always said you were left with friends."

"I thought they were friends of *maman*. I didn't know them before, but I do remember them coming to the house and taking me away to another house." She paused to sip her coffee. "I'm sorry, I was so young, and it was such a long time ago. All I have are fleeting memories. I knew them as Aunty Sheila and Uncle Bob." She shrugged. "I can't tell you more than that. I'm sorry."

Pascale sat back, processing her mother's words. She had hoped for something more concrete, but even these small, fleeting details felt like fragments of a long-hidden truth. "Did you ever think she was involved in something... dangerous? And who was this man? Can you remember anything about him? *Grand-père* was away in Africa at the time. Was that a part of the conversation? Anything? Anything at all?"

Colette's gaze flickered to the window, her thoughts drifting like the fading sunlight outside. "He was tall. Tall with light-coloured hair. Although he usually wore a hat and a raincoat. Arthur. Yes, he was called Arthur. It was a dangerous time, Pascale. No one was untouched. But your *Grand-mère*, she always seemed so... normal. Too normal. I don't know what she was protecting or running from. But, young as I was, I felt she had secrets she could never share. Arthur might not have been his real name."

Pascale nodded slowly, her mind racing with possibilities. "I just need to know, *maman*. I need to understand what happened to her after that. I don't want her legacy to remain a mystery. You said she was a teacher in England."

Colette took a deep breath, looking into Pascale's eyes. "Yes. She escaped to England with your grandfather and me when France fell. She took a job teaching languages at a school." She paused, thinking. "It was in Surrey somewhere, I remember the aircraft flying overhead."

"What type of aircraft? Can you remember?"

Colette frowned. "Good lord, after all this time, you expect me to remember details like that? Does it matter?"

"It might help to determine where you were."

"Oh, yes, I suppose so." She paused again. "Mostly, they were the small ones. Fighters. I do remember bigger ones sometimes, but they weren't so frequent."

"We can find out what aerodromes existed in Surrey. It might help us pin the location down. Likely fighter command. And *Grand-mère*, she was a teacher, you were saying?"

"Yes. She was fluent in English, Italian, and German. Maybe it's time to dig into those stories from the past. If anyone can find out what happened, it's you and Patrice. But be careful, Pascale. Some things are better left buried."

Pascale sat still, the sound of the cicadas outside the only intrusion, the weight of her mother's words sinking in. The silence stretched again, but now it felt like a moment of mutual understanding, an unspoken bond between them, tied by the mystery of a past neither of them fully knew.

"There's something I want you to see," she said eventually. "Here."

She took out Lucien Defrense's photograph. A black-and-white snapshot of a small group of men and women smiling for the camera, slightly creased and faded with time. One of them was a young woman with dark hair partially covered by a beret. Dark eyes stared out from the past. Taking the image out of her bag, she placed it gently on the table before her mother. The picture was grainy but clear enough to see the young faces, some serious, others smiling faintly, Claire Lemoine among them, looking both familiar and foreign. There was a sense of quiet defiance in her posture, as though she were hiding something even in the most casual of moments.

She pushed it across the table, and Colette picked it up.

"*Maman*," she said, her voice steady but tinged with urgency. "Lucien Defrense found this in the archives he uncovered. It was taken sometime in 1943, after Claire disappeared from England. It is her, *Grand-mère*, with others. Resistance fighters, he said." She paused, letting the words sink in. She pointed to a young man. "This is Jean-Luc Defrense, Lucien's uncle. He was there. He knew her back then, during the war." She moved her finger along the picture. "This was Jean-Luc's brother, Henri, Lucien's father, and Suzanne Moreau, the other young woman. I'm not sure where she fits in yet, but we may find something in the archives when we start searching properly."

Colette's face shifted, something unreadable flickering across her features at the mention of Lucien's name. There was a moment of hesitation before she responded, a shadow of recognition in her eyes.

"Henri Defrense?" she repeated, almost to herself. "He was a friend of your *maman's* before the war, I think? He joined up as soon as the Nazis started their blitzkrieg. But I always thought he had been killed during the fall of France."

Pascale nodded. "No, apparently not. He was killed later by the SS, according to Lucien. Lucien said he had found the photograph in the archives, so Jean-Luc and Henri survived the fall and joined the resistance movement."

Colette stared at the photograph for a long time, her fingers trembling slightly as she reached to touch it. Her lips parted, but no words emerged immediately. Finally, she spoke, her voice almost a whisper.

"I remember her smile, but this… I never saw this side of her. I didn't know, Pascale. I didn't know." Her voice broke slightly, the weight of the moment pressing down on her. She placed the photograph on the table and turned to look at the window, her gaze distant.

Pascale watched her mother closely, noting the mixture of awe and regret on her face. "Lucien said she was heavily involved, but what happened on that last mission to the Pyrenees? We don't know."

Colette looked up at Pascale, her eyes wide. "I don't know what to tell you, *Chérie*. I didn't know any of this, but Lucien, what has he found out, Pascale?"

Pascale shook her head. "Not much so far. He made the connection and discovered this photograph. That's when he came to me. His investigation doesn't appear to have gone too far. We need to find out if Jean-Luc is still alive. Then we can talk to him. But Lucien said he, too, disappeared. That was later in the war, he said. Several cell members went south on an escape run to Spain and never returned. We don't know if any of them are alive or dead. The Nazis may have executed them. Clarice will start digging through any archives she can find on the Internet. I might go to Paris. David is going to England to see if he can find anything there. He thinks SOE was involved."

Colette looked at her with a mix of pride and caution. "Just be careful, Pascale. The past can hold more than stories—it can hold dangers, too."

Pascale took the photograph back and placed it into her bag, her mind racing ahead and her determination growing. "I will, *Maman*. I have to. For *Grand-mère*."

"Before you go, there is one thing," Colette said. She went to a drawer in the kitchen dresser. "It's in here somewhere. Ah, here it is." She took out a small flat biscuit tin and put it on the table. Opening it, she took out some documents. "*Maman's* birth certificate," she said. "And some pictures taken before the war."

The room fell silent again as Pascale leafed through the items. The birth certificate would be a useful start for archive searches. The photographs showed a dark-haired woman smiling at the camera, with a baby in her arms as if there were nothing in the world to worry about. The clouds of war loomed far ahead. They lapsed into silence again as they sipped their coffee, each lost in thought. But this time, it was different—filled with a shared understanding of Pascale's impending journey. A journey that may lead her deeper into the shadows of history but also closer to the truth of who her grandmother truly was.

Colette walked with Pascale back out to the bike. "I feel as if I have been interrogated," she said with a half smile.

"*Désolé*, Patrice did warn me about that, but old habits die hard."

"Don't worry. It gave me an insight into your work. I understand how effective you can be." She smiled and kissed Pascale on the cheek. "Take care, *Chérie*."

***

As she watched her mother disappear back into the house and close the door, Pascale breathed in the waft of lavender drifting from the nearby bushes.

"Hello, Geneviève," she said.

Geneviève Duval leaned casually against the gate pillar, dressed just as she had been all those years ago when she died. It looked absurd in thirty degrees of heat, and she was wrapped in her purple winter coat and bobble hat. But it had been Christmas in northern France when she was shot and killed by Fábián Rousseau three decades ago now.

"You've got a new case," Geneviève said. "Personal this time."

"Yes. Personal."

"You never talked much about family," Geneviève went on. "All you could ever ramble on about was motorbikes and the men you fancied in the office. I never heard a word about what mattered. Yet we were friends. Colleagues for so long. You always kept your personal life fiercely private."

"You can talk. What about the English lad, Mike? You never told me you went over and spent time with him."

Geneviève grinned. "Ah, what might have been."

"I'm sorry it wasn't. But that's by the by. Why are you here?"

Geneviève shrugged. "Curiosity, in part. But also… I feel something."

"Oh, that. You always feel something. But you never give me enough to actually act on."

"You know how it works. I never get specifics, just, feelings. It's for you to decide what that might be."

"*D'accord*, madame. What is it you feel?"

"Someone wants to stop you."

"Who?"

She shook her head and shrugged.

Pascale sighed. "I tell you what, reappear when you've got something useful to say."

She pressed the starter on the bike and swung her leg over. As she lifted the machine off the sidestand, she looked back. Geneviève was gone.

Always the same, she thought. *Waste of bloody time.*

***

Leatherhead, Surrey, 1941

Claire picked up the textbooks and put them in the cupboard, ready for the next morning. The room had an empty, melancholy feel about it with the winter sunshine streaming through the taped windows, chalk motes hanging in the beams of light, and the heavy silence left behind by her departing charges.

She returned to the desk and collected the exercise books she would spend her evening marking. Routine and order had become her daily life. But that was about to change. She paused for a moment as she pondered her situation and looked around. On the walls were posters of nouns, verbs and adjectives in French, German and Italian. A pinboard proudly displayed the winning essays from the competitions she ran. This place was a home from home, and she felt a part of it.

Since Arthur Spencer had posed a new possibility, she had considered his words. It wasn't a decision she had taken lightly, but duty had a strong call.

She walked across the playground. It was empty now. The children had all gone home. At the gate, he stood. Just as she had expected, he wanted his answer.

As she turned out of the gate and trod the familiar path home, he stepped alongside her, smoking a cigarette, saying nothing as they walked. The air was filled with a damp autumnal smell. Somewhere, she caught the faint aroma of woodsmoke beneath the tobacco smoke of Spencer's cigarette. The mulch from the fallen leaves was slippery underfoot, and she instinctively pulled her heavy wool coat closer to her body. Eventually, they were almost at the gate to her lodgings.

She stopped and looked at him, his eyes partially concealed by the brim of his fedora.

"You haven't asked," she said.

He flicked the end of the cigarette to the ground and smiled as he crushed it beneath his heel.

"I'm a patient man."

"So I see."

She looked about. Across the green, the tops of the trees were stark in their winter guise, and the crows squawked and fluttered against the bright sky, their cries carrying on the still air, the leaves long since fallen, leaving branches like naked fingers reaching up to the heavens. The Oxshott woods were an anchor in the wild seas that engulfed the world around her, and she hoped one day to see them again.

"What if I said 'no'?"

He shrugged. "Then we would have tried. I can't persuade people against their will. I don't conscript like the army. It doesn't work that way. You have to want to go. Be prepared to take the risks. Be prepared, if necessary, to make the ultimate sacrifice."

"But you do that to soldiers."

"Different. Operating every day behind enemy lines requires volunteers. If you're not one hundred per cent certain, then I'm not interested. You wouldn't survive out there. *Couldn't* survive."

He lapsed into silence, and they locked eyes for a moment.

"One hundred per cent?" she said.

"Yes. Nothing less."

"*Vive la France*," she said. "Is that answer enough?"

He nodded. "I'll be in contact with arrangements."

She watched him go.

Life was about to take a very different, very dangerous turn.

Chapter 4

Crieff, 1921

James Kerr arrived home from school. He was small for his age, and his sandy hair, blue eyes, and rounded face made him look much younger than he was. As on previous occasions, his uniform was scuffed, his knees were skinned, and a darkening bruise bloomed over his left eye. His mother, Hanna, opened the door and looked at her son.

"Again?"

"Don't worry about it, Ma. I'm fine."

"You are not fine, *Liebling*."

"That's the problem, Ma. We're Germans, and they hate me for it. You speaking German doesn't help. I wish you wouldn't."

Hanna sighed. "I'm sorry. It's who I am. I cannot change that. Come in. There's someone I want you to meet."

They entered the sitting room, where a middle-aged man in a dark coat and fedora hat sat smoking a cigarette. He wore a small military-style moustache that curled slightly at the ends, the grey stained yellow by nicotine. James thought he saw sadness in the man's demeanour. His eyes seemed distant, shadowed by a grief James couldn't place, as he stood and extended a hand with a brief, polite smile. James took the proffered hand and watched as the man spoke.

"I am Herr Otto Reinhardt, James. Like your father, I fought in the war," he shrugged slightly. "Albeit on the other side. Still, I sympathise with the situation you now find yourself in. There were good men on both sides, and we all recognise those who died bravely for their country. Your father was an admirable man, boy." He gestured for James to sit. "I represent an organisation in Germany. We are called the *Kulturverein für Heimkehr*. We aim to support German families abroad, helping them find a place in the new Germany."

"What kind of place?"

"A good school, a new start. Somewhere you'll belong."

"We barely have enough for bread these days, with the prices so high after the war. I don't know how much longer we can stay here," Hanna said.

"Germany suffered after Versailles, James. We're helping her heal, starting with families like yours."

"And what do you do, exactly, Herr Reinhardt?"

Reinhardt smiled as he sat back down and stubbed his cigarette in the ashtray. "As I said, we are rebuilding Germany and looking for young Germans to be part of that future. Your mother is a German living in what has become a hostile land. And you, well, I see the bruises. I can offer you something different. A place at a German school. A home. And," he paused, "I can help you with the bullies, for you will still find them in Germany. They are everywhere, and we teach boys how to fight back. Would you like that?"

James stood quietly, studying the man. Reinhardt, unbothered, opened a silver cigarette case and took out a fresh cigarette with casual elegance, though James noticed a slight tremble as he fiddled with it, fumbling almost. Reinhardt ran a thumb over the engraved initials, a flicker of something. Nostalgia, perhaps, crossed his face.

"What does A.K. stand for?" James asked, eyeing the engraved initials.

Reinhardt paused, his gaze sharpening slightly. Then he smiled faintly. "*Alles klar*," he said. "*Alles klar*. My late wife used to say it, and it stuck. In our society, it means we're ready. Everything is clear for the future."

"I see," said James. "*Alles klar*."

Reinhardt chuckled at the boy's echo. "You haven't answered my question, boy."

James briefly looked across to the mantelpiece, where a photograph of his father looked out in sepia-toned formality in his fresh uniform before going to war in 1914. A father he had barely known, yet he was tainted with the blood of the enemy that had killed him. James swallowed as he looked, his fists clenched briefly at his sides. "I think I just did, Herr Reinhardt," he said.

Reinhardt looked at Hanna, one brow lifting slightly.

"I told you," she said. "He's mature for his age."

Reinhardt rose and buttoned his coat, the cigarette case glinting in his pocket as he turned to leave. "Well then, *Frau* Kerr, I will arrange for you to receive the necessary documents and travel details. I'll be in touch."

***

Frankfurt 1924

James Kerr was walking home from school when a small group of boys blocked his path.

Not again.

He stopped and looked at Heinrich Vogel, a fair-skinned, dark-haired young man, and solidly built for his age. James had seen him around the school. They were in different classes, so didn't mix much, but Vogel often repeated comments that were gaining traction, Germany for the Germans, and dark mentions of the *untermensch*. He hadn't said anything directly to James, but his half-English heritage was frowned upon by this boy, so James had made a point of keeping his distance. Now, it seemed, that tactic was not going to work.

"English," Vogel said with a sneer, standing directly in James' way. "Go home, we don't want you here."

James stood his ground, his body relaxed.

"Did you hear me, English?"

"I'm a German, as much as you are."

"You will never be as I am, English." He stepped forward, pushing James firmly on the shoulder. James moved back, absorbing the shove while letting his school bag slip from his shoulder and drop to the ground. Sensing blood, the group crowded in.

"Fight! Fight!"

Vogel swung his fist in a haymaker, and James ducked it cleanly, lifting his fists to protect his face, elbows in. James stepped under the blow as Vogel came in for another strike, launching a right jab to the solar plexus. Vogel whooped with pain and curled forward to meet the left hook that connected with his jaw. As he staggered back, James brought another right jab to his face, causing Vogel's legs to buckle, and he fell to the ground. Winded, he gazed at James. "I didn't know you could fight, Yahmes."

"Maybe you should have asked." He stepped forward and extended a hand, grabbing Vogel's arm and helping him to his feet. "Never underestimate your opponent, Heinrich."

A surge of confidence and a flicker of guilt ran through him. He'd protected himself, but at what cost?

"I will remember that," Vogel said, reaching up to the bloody cut on his forehead that would leave a lifelong scar.

As James watched Vogel and his cronies walk off, he reflected on Otto Reinhardt's insistence that he take boxing lessons.

"The problems you had in Scotland with your mixed heritage won't entirely go away, my boy, but we will teach you how to fight back," he had said. "It'll serve you well for the future I see for you."

That investment had paid off. He picked up his school bag and walked away.

***

London Stanstead, Present Day

Upon hearing of his plans to travel to England, Laurence, as Clarice predicted, had decided that she would accompany him.

"It's been a long time since I went to London," she said. "We can see the sights when you are not digging around in old archives."

Clarice was tasked with looking after the dogs, and they caught a flight from Béziers to London.

The descent into London Stansted was smooth, but the moment the plane touched down, David Radfield felt the familiar weight of travel settle on his shoulders, not to mention the lurch in his stomach. He instinctively reached out to the back of the seat in front to brace himself, eliciting a smile from Laurence, who remained unruffled by the experience.

"I hate flying," he once said. "Bloody unnatural."

"So, why do you do it, *mon cher?*"

"Necessity," he said, glowering at her gentle teasing. He loved this woman with all his heart, but by God, she knew which buttons to press.

The interminable shuffle from tarmac to baggage reclaim was its own brand of purgatory that always reminded him why he'd chosen the quiet, brown countryside of the Larzac over the frenetic pace of a city like London, or even his own hometown of Bristol, where the hustle of the city centre had never suited him. The impersonal sprawl of Stansted's terminal stood in stark contrast to the small, localised affair of Béziers-Cap d'Agde Airport, where you could be off the plane and on your way in minutes. The crowds pressed in from all sides, a cacophony of voices, the odour of sweat and pungent perfume, tinny announcements, and the clatter of rolling suitcases banging his shins, assaulting his senses, and he felt his jaw tense.

Radfield gripped Laurence Gunthier's hand tightly as they navigated the throng, her presence a steadying anchor amidst the chaos. She glanced at him, her expression a mix of amusement and sympathy, sensing his discomfort. They collected their bags from the reclaim belt. His was a battered leather holdall that had seen years of sterling service, while hers was a sleek roller case, and they made their way through immigration, the line was mercifully short for once. Finally, they entered the crisp spring air, the terminal noise and smells fading behind them.

Radfield exhaled, feeling the tension in his shoulders ease slightly. He led Laurence along the cab line, flagging down a black taxi and giving the driver the address of their hotel in Kew. The cabbie, a wiry man with a weathered face, raised an eyebrow as he loaded their bags into the boot.

"This one won't be cheap, mate," he said. "Long drive from here to the other side of London."

Radfield nodded, his tone clipped but polite. "I know, but it's less hassle than the train, just get us there, thanks."

"Very good, guv."

Laurence squeezed his hand, her eyes bright with anticipation. "I will enjoy coming back to London," she said, her subtle French accent stirring something in him even in this mundane environment. Radfield's mind drifted for a moment, a wave of gratitude washing over him as he thought about how lucky his life had been to have met this woman. He made a mental note to thank Pascale for that opportunity. Her detective agency had brought them together, after all.

"Even if it is a business trip," Laurence added, unaware of his drifting attention.

Radfield gave a wry smile, his mood lifting at her enthusiasm. "Sure, and the sooner I'm on a flight back to France, the better I'll like it."

She rolled her eyes playfully and nudged his arm. "Sometimes, David, you can be a real bundle of joy."

He grinned, the first genuine smile since they'd landed. "I can, can't I?"

They settled into the back of the cab, the city unfolding beyond the windows as the driver pulled into traffic and headed down the M1 toward the North Circular. Laurence leaned against him, her head resting lightly on his shoulder, and Radfield placed a hand on hers, letting himself relax for a moment. The hum of the engine was a soothing counterpoint to the earlier chaos, the steady rhythm grounding him as the cab navigated the familiar arteries of London.

"So, what are we doing tomorrow?" Laurence asked, her voice soft but curious.

"The National Archives," Radfield said, his mind already shifting to the task ahead. "I want to see what they throw up about SOE and whether Claire Lemoine was recruited here. Anything else will be a bonus."

Laurence nodded, her fingers tracing absent patterns on his hand. "Then we'll find what Pascale needs," she said with quiet confidence. "And maybe a little time for us, too. I want to do a little sightseeing."

Radfield chuckled, pressing a kiss to her forehead. "That, we can manage."

As the cab wound its way through the outskirts of London, Radfield's thoughts turned to the archives waiting in Kew. Somewhere in those records was the truth about Claire Lemoine, Flamme, and he was determined to uncover it, for Pascale and for the legacy of a woman who'd fought in the shadows.

Chapter 5

Kew, Present Day

David Radfield and Laurence Gunthier walked through Kew to the modern façade of the National Archives building. They made their way to the main reception.

"David Radfield," he said when they reached the reception desk. "I called ahead."

"Ah, yes, please, follow me." They followed the receptionist through to the reading room. "If you wait here, someone will be along with what you asked for."

A few minutes later, a young woman came in carrying a pile of folders.

"These are the military and intelligence records from 1941 to 1942."

"Thank you. We will start here."

"What exactly are you looking for, Mr. Radfield?"

"Anything we can find on a Claire Lemoine. She was a language teacher, and we believe SOE recruited her."

The woman nodded. "Have you tried school records from the Ministry of Education or local recruitment offices that dealt with language instructors? Those with teaching experience in foreign languages would have been prime candidates for recruitment. There would have been local scouts who would have approached her."

"Excellent idea, miss…"

"Sorry," she held out a hand. "Yvonne Saunders, I'm a senior archivist here. It was me you spoke to on the phone."

"Of course. Yes, I recognise the voice. If you can point us to the educational records, that would help. The only detail we've got, from her daughter's vague memories, is that she taught somewhere in the south. Near a Spitfire aerodrome, possibly. At least, that is the best we can deduce given that the witness was very young at the time."

"What if I look at the educational records, and you concentrate on the military ones," Laurence said.

"You might have to go to the local records offices," Yvonne said. However, I will look into what I can from here and let you browse those."

She paused. "If I may ask…"

"Ask away," Radfield said.

"What is this about? What are you looking for?"

Radfield smiled. "My colleague is trying to discover what happened to her grandmother. We have a few snippets of information. She disappeared in France. However, her daughter lost touch with her here. I am trying to find out if she was recruited by SOE. I'm following an old policeman's hunch."

"Of course. Well, I will see if I can find the relevant education records for you."

She walked back to her office and sat down. She paused for a moment before picking up the phone. She dialled and listed. A man answered.

"Yes?"

"It's me. You said that someone might come looking for information on Claire Lemoine."

"And?"

"They are here. An Englishman and a French woman. They're going through the records now. What are they looking for that you need to know about?"

"Never mind that. Just give them what they ask for. Don't call me again. If I need to, I'll call you."

The phone went dead, and she looked at it momentarily as if it would answer her unspoken questions. Eventually, she left the office and went to the educational records to find what Laurence had requested.

***

They lost track of time while poring over the files. It was Laurence who found something first. "Here, David, I've found something."

He walked over to the desk where she was working. "What?"

She pointed to the record: "A teacher in Leatherhead called Claire Lemoine. That's our woman, isn't it?"

Radfield grinned. "That's her. We need to dig a bit deeper down in Surrey, then. In the meantime, I need to keep looking through these SOE records. If she was there, I'll find her."

It was some while later when he found what he was looking for. A record of an operative code-named Flamme. "Recruited in 1941," he said. "I'll need some more on that." He looked at his watch. "It's getting late. We should be going back to the hotel and come back tomorrow."

It was late afternoon when they left the National Archives and returned through Kew along Ruskin Avenue, turning into Mortlake Road. Their eyes scanned the street, waiting for an opportunity to cross. The crossing signal changed, and Radfield started stepping onto the road. They heard the screech of tyres, and before they could fully process what was happening, a black BMW car swerved toward them, engine revving as the driver accelerated hard.

Laurence reacted first, grabbing Radfield by the arm and yanking him back onto the pavement. They barely cleared the vehicle's path as it hurtled past, narrowly missing them by inches. They ran back towards the corner of Ruskin Avenue, making their way back in the direction of the National Archives building.

"We need to call someone," Radfield said, breathing heavily. "Come on, quickly now." They heard the driver revving and changing gear as the car swung around, now directly in pursuit.

Radfield's breath came in short bursts as his mind raced. He looked across at Laurence, whose face was pale and drawn. As he processed the implications, he now understood the game's rules: They were not just searching for a piece of history. They had uncovered something, or someone, that powerful forces were desperate to keep hidden.

"That was no coincidence," he said. "We've stirred up something that someone wants kept buried."

"God, I can't run in these shoes," Laurence said, pausing long enough to kick them off and grab them by the straps. "I'm okay; keep going," she panted.

"And I'm too old to be doing this. I thought I'd retired from this nonsense," he said between gasps.

They ran, the adrenaline kicking in, Radfield's mind a blur, but the instinct to survive kicked in. He grabbed Laurence's arm again, urging her to keep running. The BMW was now directly behind them as they reached the gates of the Archives.

"Quick, let us in," Redfield said to the security guard. Fortunately, the man saw what was happening and opened the gate, slamming it shut behind them.

"I'll call the police," he said, picking up his phone. "You two better get inside and wait."

As they looked back, the BMW was turning and disappearing back the way it had come.

"Did you get the plate?" the security guard said.

"Yes," Radfield said. "But I doubt it will help. Either the car is stolen, or the plate will have been cloned. We've upset someone. Someone prepared to kill to keep a secret."

***

Lodève, Present Day

Pascale Herve sat at her desk, her fingers idly tracing the edge of a half-filled cup of coffee, her thoughts adrift. The sounds of the street outside filtered through the half-open window, but inside, there was only the weight of silence pressing against her. She'd been waiting for something from Radfield, but so far they had heard nothing. Patrice had booked tickets for Paris on the following morning's train, so until then, she was at a dead end.

However, there was something she needed to do. Putting the coffee cup down, she rose and put on her jacket. Clarice looked up from her screen with one eyebrow raised.

"I'm going out for a few minutes," Pascale said. "Something I have to do."

Clarice nodded and went back to her work.

Once outside, Pascale mounted the FTR and rode the short distance through the town, stopping briefly at the flower shop at the bottom of the town before heading out to the cemetery.

She parked the bike at the gates and walked along the gravel pathway, eventually stopping at one of the graves.

"Hello, Guillaume," she said. She crouched down, pulled away the dried flowers, and picked bits of litter that had swept in on the wings of the Mistral. Absorbed with her task, she didn't notice Geneviève appear beside her.

"He would have been sixty today," Geneviève said, standing hands in pockets as she watched Pascale in her task.

Pascale sat back on her haunches and looked up. "I know. I have a few years to go yet. Sometimes, I think I am the only one who remembers."

"Patrice knows," Geneviève said. "He will be along shortly."

Pascale finished arranging the flowers as she liked and walked across to the regular bench where she sat and pondered the meaning of life and death during her moments of solitude.

"What are you working on now?" Geneviève said.

"*Grand-mère* Lemoine still."

"Everything going as planned?"

Pascale gave her a sharp look. "Has anything come of your cryptic warning, you mean?"

"Yes, that."

"Not so far, no."

"And the investigation?"

Pascale sighed. "After all these years, I may discover what happened to her. Lay a ghost to rest." She looked across at Geneviève. "Although I never seem to have laid you to rest."

You may need to tread carefully," Geneviève said. "Some ghosts do not want to be disturbed."

Pascale leaned back against the bench. "What are you telling me? Will someone stop us? Like you said the other day?"

"Yes. Be careful. You may be treading a dangerous path."

Her phone rang, breaking the stillness, and she jolted, her pulse quickening. She answered it, her voice steady but strained.

"David, how is it going in London?"

"Pascale. Something has happened," he paused, and she tensed as she sensed the tension in his voice.

"What?" she said.

Geneviève stared passively into the distance.

"We found some evidence of your grandmother's past. I'll send that through, but as Laurence and I were making our way back to the hotel, someone tried to kill us."

She looked again at Geneviève, but she was alone on the bench. *Typical*, she thought.

"You're sure?"

She heard the scrunch of footsteps and looked up as Patrice walked over with a bouquet of flowers. He stopped and placed them on the grave before looking towards her. He saw the look on her face as she gestured for him to come closer. He sat down beside her.

She turned on the phone's loudspeaker. "Patrice is listening in, David. What happened?"

"A car tried to run into us."

"You are sure it wasn't an accident?"

"No. Having missed, they turned around and came back after us. We were targeted. No question about it. It looks as if we have two investigations on our hands."

Pascale's breath caught in her throat, and her grip tightened on the phone. "How do you know? Who is it?"

"Doesn't matter," Radfield said. "Someone is upset by this investigation. Have you spoken to Lucien Defrense since he came to the office?"

"No, but I think we might have to delay our trip to Paris." She looked across at Patrice, who nodded.

Pascale felt a cold tingle down her spine and something lurched in her stomach, but she knew better than to let it take hold. Her mind raced, searching for answers, piecing together the fragments of information they'd gathered. What had seemed a straightforward look into her family history was now dangerous.

"What are you going to do now?" Pascale asked, her voice betraying no hint of the turmoil within. "If you decide to stop and come back, I will understand."

Radfield laughed, but it was more a bark than a genuine laugh. "When have I let a little thing like a death threat stop me? I am concerned about Laurence, though. I think she should come back." Pascale heard a voice in the background, and Radfield came back onto the phone. "Apparently not," he said. "Anyway, we have found Claire's SOE records. We are going to Leatherhead tomorrow to speak to someone down there, although I suspect we have most of what we need for the moment. Anything that the people at Leatherhead can tell us will be useful background."

"David, be careful."

"Don't worry about us. We will be fine."

The line went dead. Pascale put the phone back into her pocket and looked across at Patrice.

"What do you think?"

"I think Radfield will look after himself and Laurence. I also think we need to get to Nîmes and see Defrense. Something is going on here that we don't know about, and I suspect he knows more than he let on the other day."

"*D'accord*, I agree. I had a feeling at the time."

They got up to walk back to the road. Pascale looked back at the bench. Geneviève sat smiling. She lifted a finger to her forehead in a salute.

***

Nîmes, Present Day

Patrice drove, and Pascale sat silently in the passenger seat as they travelled from Lodève to Nîmes. The autoroute was quiet at this time of day, and the sun baked the land, turning it a dun brown colour. Patrice kept the air conditioning on inside the car, and Pascale sat back, enjoying blast of cool air from the dashboard on her face, a welcome contrast to the baking heat outside.

On the outskirts of Nîmes, they followed the D40 until it intersected with the D926, then turned onto Mas de Guiraudon. They turned left onto a tree-lined road dotted with small, detached houses featuring white stucco walls and red-tiled roofs, each accompanied by swimming pools, shimmering in the harsh Mediterranean light.

"It should be up here somewhere," Patrice said, leaning forward and peering through the windscreen.

"Uh, oh."

As he spoke, they saw the police cars flashing blue lights and the road barricaded off with tape. Patrice stopped the car, and they walked over to the agent de police standing by the tape.

"You cannot go any further, monsieur-dame," he said firmly, hand resting on his radio.

Pascale frowned. "We were coming to see Monsieur Defrense. He lives here."

The agent's tone changed subtly, softening as he spoke. "I'm sorry, madame. Did you know Monsieur Defrense?"

Pascale sighed. "Briefly. He came to us for help. We are private detectives. He was researching his family history."

The agent reached for his radio. "I will call the *capitaine*, madame. He will want to talk to you."

A few moments later, *Capitaine* François Viala walked out of the house and down the driveway to meet them.

"Well," he said, with a weary smile of recognition on his face. "It seems to me that you two always manage to arrive at one of my crime scenes. What brings you here this time?"

Pascale repeated what she had just told the agent.

"You had better come and look," Viala said, lifting the tape and gesturing for them to follow. They walked into the house. Inside, the house was cool and quiet despite the professional business of the investigative team gathering their evidence. In the front room, Defrense's body lay face up on the floor. His face was pale with blueish lips, eyes wide open, staring sightlessly at the ceiling.

"His neighbour called in this morning and found him lying here," Viala said. "Apparently, she gets his bread for him from the boulangerie. She saw him like this and called us immediately."

Patrice nodded and crouched down to examine the scene closely. "It looks like a heart attack, so why are you involved, François?"

The pathologist watched the exchange and inclined his head. Viala nodded. He crouched down beside Patrice. "That's my initial suspicion, Patrice. However, I'm not certain," he said.

"I cannot be sure about the cause of death until I get him back to the lab," the pathologist said.

"Do you suspect something other than natural causes?"

"I am sending samples to toxicology, but until then, I am not saying. However, someone else was here. The body had been moved and what looks bruises on the chest that could be post-mortem, yet there were no unusual fingerprints. Whoever was here was forensically aware and cleared up afterwards."

"How odd," Patrice said. "Anyone see anything?"

"A neighbour saw a black Citroën pulling away about the right time, but didn't get a plate."

Patrice stood and frowned. "So," Pascale said. "You have a death that is both suspicious, but probably natural? Is that it?"

"Yes, that's about it," Viala said. "There is evidence that someone was here when this man died, yet made no attempt to call for help. Something is off here, and I don't like it."

They walked back out to the cars, and the agent lifted the tape for them to pass through. Viala paused. "Whatever your investigation, this is now a police matter. At least until I rule out foul play."

"That may be so," Pascale said. "However, our investigation is relevant. There is no reason why we cannot continue with that and keep you informed while you find out what happened to Monsieur Defrense."

Patrice took a deep breath. "Pascale *Chérie,* what about the attempt on David and Laurence?"

Viala stiffened slightly. "Please, tell."

They told him about Radfield's excursion to the National Archives and the attempt on their lives.

"I think," Patrice said, "this goes beyond just your jurisdiction, François."

"We have ruffled some feathers, I think," Pascale said.

"All the more reason to leave it alone and let us investigate."

Pascale shook her head. "François, you can only investigate here. This goes wider. I think it's best if we carry on with our research into my grandmother's past and you investigate Monsieur Defrense's death. We will keep you informed of anything relevant."

Viala looked at her, meeting her eyes.

"You won't take 'no' for an answer, will you?"

Pascale smiled and shook her head.

"I thought not. Nothing changes, eh?"

"Nothing changes."

"Be careful."

"Of course."

Viala sighed and watched them go. Once in the car, Pascale turned to Patrice. "Paris?"

"Paris," he said.

***

Pierrefitte-sur-Seine, Present Day

After an uneventful rail journey and an overnight stop in a hotel, Pascale and Patrice arrived at the *Archives Nationales*, a modern building that sprawled over a section of land near the N1. They parked the rental car outside and headed for the reception desk, their footsteps echoing on the tiled floor. They walked in silence. The tension from Defrense's death and the attempt on Radfield and Laurence hung unspoken in the air. Pascale reached out for Patrice's hand, and he wrapped his fingers around hers and smiled at her.

After a quick check-in at the reception desk, they were handed visitor badges and directed to the reading rooms. Among the rows of researchers hunched over old manuscripts and microfiche machines, they found a quiet space, much as Radfield had done in London a few days earlier. A staff member pointed them to the relevant section containing wartime documents and Resistance files. The archives were divided by themes, and the Resistance records were tucked away in a carefully preserved section.

Pascale's eyes scanned the shelves of bound volumes while Patrice flipped through a reference guide. Finding the right file wouldn't be easy. But they had one lead: Claire Lemoine's name. Thanks to the birth certificate, they had an age, and she was involved in the Resistance. What they didn't know was where she was based.

"A good starting point," Patrice said, "will be the *Fichiers des Personnalités* and the *Dossiers de la Résistance*."

They went to a large wooden desk and spoke to a staff member who requested specific files. Moments later, they were handed folders marked with the names of Resistance groups, informant lists, and various records of operations.

"Now we start," Pascale said as she opened one of the files. They spent the next few hours poring over the documents.

"*D'accord*," Pascale said. "I have found some references. *Grand-mère* worked in an intelligence network that helped smuggle people out of occupied France. Here, there are references to coded messages she sent and her work with a cell known as '*La Libération*, in Rouen,' although" she paused and looked up. "The details are a little sparse. Some of the information about her activities has been classified or redacted."

Patrice came across and looked over her shoulder. "Maybe that is to protect anyone who is still alive. That said, the youngest would be in their nineties by now."

One document caught their attention: a letter dated July 1943, written by a high-ranking Resistance leader. "This person's name has been redacted," she swore. "This is proving hard. But this is interesting."

The letter described Claire Lemoine's role as a guide for allied airmen making their way to Spain, though it remained vague about how she achieved this without being caught. The letter mentioned her bravery, strong leadership, and ability to move between undetected regions. "Look, here. There is a reference to an SOE agent. She is in close contact. But no information about who it was."

Patrice looked at the document and ran his finger along the page as he read. "Oh, it's more than that, *Chérie*. She was running an agent. Now that is interesting and unexpected."

Excited but frustrated by the lack of more detailed information, Pascale and Patrice took notes and decided to request more files, hoping that the key to understanding the full scope of Claire's contributions lay somewhere in these vast archives. Yet what was emerging was that she played a key part in the command structure.

"Here," Pascale said, "extracts from a journal."

Patrice came across and read it over his shoulder.

"There's a lot that has been redacted," he said, "And here she talks about the training she had before she was deployed."

"I wonder what that was like?"

"Oh, God, it was brutal. They were put through some intensive psychological stuff, from what I understand. Then, weapons training and radio. They had to be able to send Morse code at something like eighteen words per minute. All in about six weeks from start to finish, and most of them didn't last long in the field. Life expectancy was a matter of weeks."

"It's hard to imagine what it was like."

***

Wanborough Manor, 1941

When would they come back?

The room was dark. Just the desk lamp. No windows. No clock. Hours or days? It felt like weeks. What was the last thing she could remember?

That was it. They'd asked for ID. Said it was forged. Wouldn't believe her.

Who sent her?

Where had she come from?

They hadn't believed her answers. Over and over, the same questions. Same responses.

She gave the cover story. Repeated it. They didn't believe it. Same questions. Over and over.

How long had it been? She didn't know.

She hadn't slept.

Focus. Keep calm. Focus.

How long had they been gone this time? Minutes? An hour?

Spencer. He'd brought her here. Wanborough Manor. Not far from Leatherhead.

She'd said goodbye to Colette. Then the car. An hour or so's drive.

How long ago had that been? She blinked. Her throat was dry. The door opened. She jumped.

Spencer.

"Very good, Mrs Lemoine."

Her eyes narrowed. "Who are you talking to? I don't know a Mrs Lemoine. Never heard of her."

Spencer smiled.

The overhead lights came on. He placed a folder on the desk.

"You can go back to your quarters now, Claire. This exercise is over."

She stared at him. Was it? Could she believe that?

Trust no one. Trust nothing. Not even him.

Another man entered. Cold, unreadable.

"That exercise is now finished," he said. "We'll let you know later how you did."

He opened the door. "You're free to go."

She stood slowly, warily. Legs stiff. Breath shallow.

Was this still part of it?

She stepped into the corridor. No one followed. No orders. No guards. Just silence.

Back in her room, she sat down on the bed. Looked at the door. Waited.

Still nothing.

She rubbed her face with shaking hands.

"Bastards," she muttered.

Weapons Training, Arisaig House, Scottish Highlands, 1941

Chief Petty Officer Freddie McTaggart, Royal Navy, glared at his charges. His grey eyes bored into each of them as if daring to expose their very souls. The room was sparse and functional, and the sweet, metallic odour of gun oil pervaded the atmosphere.

"Civilians with guns scare the shit out of me," he said. "The thought of you lot poncing about in France with firearms must give Jerry the fucking willies. I almost feel sorry for the bastards."

It struck Claire that he didn't sound very sorry. But she kept that to herself. No one else said a word.

He picked up a Luger P08 and held it so the group could all see.

"Before we start, two golden rules. Number one: When the weapon is not in use, the safety catch is to be on at all times. "Am I clear?"

"Yes, chief," they said almost in unison.

"Number two: You do *not* point a weapon, loaded or not, at another person. If I catch anyone doing that, you are off this course, *toot sweet*. Am I clear?"

"Yes, chief."

"Good. When the time comes to use a weapon in anger and you are pointing it at another person, you shoot to kill, 'cause it will be them or you. Make sure it's them. Clear?"

"Yes, chief."

He fixed his stare on each delegate in turn, allowing the weight of his words to sink home. Then he lifted the Luger again, holding it like it was an extension of his body.

"This, ladies and gentlemen, is the Luger P08. A nine-millimetre Parabellum with a magazine holding eight rounds. It's well balanced," he said, weighing it in his hand. "Safety's on the side here, and it's bloody accurate. Excellent pistol," he paused, "even if it is made by Jerry. One shortfall is that the bugger can jam if it gets mucky, so you lot will learn how to keep your new best friend so spick and span I can eat my breakfast off it. Am I clear?"

They nodded. "Clear, Chief."

Claire stifled a smile at the thought of CPO McTaggart eating his breakfast off the Luger. He caught her eye and glowered, and she realised her smile hadn't gone unnoticed.

"This little thing will save your life. You need to learn how to pull it apart and put it back together. When you can strip this blighter in your sleep, and reassemble it with your eyes shut. Then and only then, you can learn how to shoot it."

So began the drills.

They took the weapons apart and immediately reassembled them. Then again. And again. And again. As they worked, their fingers grew sore, and the action became muscle memory. When one of the trainees fumbled and dropped the magazine, McTaggart barked at him.

"You're dead, sonny. Jerry just killed you while you were fannying about. Do it again."

On the range, Claire held the weapon. It felt heavy in her hands, alien, awkward, and clumsy at first.

McTaggart stood behind her, coaching her through it.

"Gentle but firm," he said. "Brace yourself for the recoil."

She pulled the trigger. The discharge cracked like thunder.

"Merde!"

The Luger kicked back hard, jarring her arms, nearly clipping her face.

At one point, she was rebuked with a sharp slap across the back of the head.

"When you aren't using it, keep the bloody safety on, got it?"

"Got it, sir."

"Don't forget it, and it's Chief. 'Sir' is for those poncy officer types."

"Yes, Chief."

He grinned. "Good. Now, again. Properly."

Once they'd mastered the Luger, they moved on to the Sten.

The same relentless rhythm. Take it apart. Put it back together. Clear a jam. Quickly. Change magazines under pressure. Learn its flaws, its temperament. Learn to trust it. Just not too much.

By the time Claire completed her weapons training, the schoolteacher she had once been felt like someone else entirely. Another life, another place, another time.

***

Wireless Training, STS 52 (Thames Valley), 1941

Then came the Morse code. Endless dots and dashes. Their instructor, Royal Signals Sergeant Jonny Sykes, spoke softly as he coached them through it.

"You're not listening for dots and dashes," he said. "It's a rhythm. Stop consciously trying to hear the characters. Let the rhythm flow. Let your hand record them subconsciously. Don't think. Feel the code move through you and don't try to read what you've written."

They sat in a room, close yet apart, separated by headphones that cut them off from one another. There were a few muttered curses when they missed a character.

"Don't worry, keep going," Sykes said. "If you get angry, the flow goes. Stay calm. Stay relaxed."

When sending, Claire had to learn how to loosen her wrist, resting her forearm and elbow on the desk with an easy, fluid motion.

"Again," Jonny said. "Flow. It's a poem. A song. A sonata. Just relax, and let it go."

"What if I miss a character?"

"Forget it. If you try to chase it, you'll miss the next one. And the next. Just leave a gap and keep moving. With practice, the gaps close. I'm looking for consistency.

Gaps are fine, for now. But then we get faster. I want twenty words a minute out of you lot. Got it?"

"Got it, Sarge."

The repetition took over her waking and sleeping life. Dots and dashes danced in her head even when her eyes were closed. But slowly, steadily, her accuracy and speed improved.

Eventually, that twenty-words-per-minute target stopped being a wall. It became a rhythm, a hum in the back of her mind. She could hear a stream of code and switch off her conscious thoughts, transcribing each character without thinking.

***

Pierrefitte-sur-Seine, Present Day

"It was a different time, the training was harsh," Patrice was saying. "Not everyone made the grade," he said, looking over Pascale's shoulder as she scanned through the fragmented document.

"What does the journal say?"

She read the entry aloud.

"Finished basic training. Very tough. I can kill a man with my bare hands. I can shoot, transcribe Morse code, send and receive at twenty words a minute. I can jump out of an aircraft and assume a new identity. What happened to the schoolteacher in Leatherhead? The past is a different place now."

She looked up from the microfiche and met his gaze in silence. He peered over her shoulder at the journal. "But this entry mentions Vanguard. That must be the agent we were reading about in that letter."

"Let me see," Pascale said. She scrolled down to the relevant entry.

'The rain had started by the time I reached Café Lys Noir. The hem of my skirt was soaked. I kept my head down. A man passed. His coat was too fine, his shoes too

clean. Not local. I tensed. Gestapo. Maybe an agent. I waited until he turned the corner, then pushed open the door.

Inside, it smelled of smoke, damp wool and burned coffee. I nodded to Églantine and went upstairs. The back room. The light barely reached the desk. I sat and waited.

Vanguard was already there. waiting. He sat in the chair by the window, looking down at the street. No greeting, no hesitation. His hat cast a shadow over his face. Only the line of his mouth was visible. I have never seen his face. Always dark places. Always the hat pulled low. Unspeaking. Unsure if I was followed.

"You are late," he said.

"There was a patrol. And a man outside. Not local."

He nodded. "I saw him. Gestapo."

He reached into his coat and handed me an envelope. It was damp from the rain, and I felt its weight before slipping it into my coat pocket.

"The Clos-Léon safe house. It is compromised."

"Merde!" The safe house was lost. "When?"

"Two days ago. Before you arrived"

"Orage said something..."

"Yes."

"Who?"

His jaw tightened. "It does not matter. Three operatives are now lost."

It did matter. But he would not say. Not yet.

"You move the airmen you still have tonight," he said. "Papers are inside. They will pass."

No question. No debate. I nodded. He stood and was gone. I waited five minutes.

Outside, the rain had turned to mist. The blackout made it difficult to see. I pulled my coat close and stepped into the dark.

There was work to do.'

"Three operatives lost, just like that. It sounds so, clinical. But it can't have been. I cannot imagine how it was for them."

***

Clos-Léon Safe House, Rouen, Winter, 1941

Matelot, Vigneron, and Renard placed their bicycles at the back of the house. The alley was deserted, and they looked around. No sign of German patrols.

"Come on."

Matelot opened the door and went in, catching the musty, damp odour that permeated the walls. In any other circumstances, the building would have been condemned, but these were days when any empty building would have to make do. He was followed by the other two. With the shutters closed, the rooms were dark, and the three airmen were shadows, sitting, waiting. They were weary and tense from the long wait, and one of them got up when he saw them.

"About time," he said. They had already dressed in the casual work clothes expected of itinerant workers, ready to move south to Spain.

"*Désolé*," Matelot said. "There are patrols everywhere, and we have to be careful."

"This place stinks," the airman said. We'll be glad to get out of here."

"Well, get ready to move, Monsieur," Matelot said. "We have your papers."

He moved to each man, handing out the *cartes d'identité* and an *Ausweis* for each.

"*D'accord*, get ready to move."

He stopped, cocking his head slightly and frowning.

"What?" the airman said.

"Shh!" Matelot raised an arm. "Listen!"

Outside, came the sudden screech of trucks pulling to a halt. Then a voice over a hailer:

"Inside the house, come out slowly with your hands raised, and no harm will come to you. You are surrounded. There is no escape."

"*Merde*," Matelot said.

"What now?" Vigneron asked, eyes wide. Matelot could see the terror coursing through her. Since that first meeting with Fournier, they had half expected this... yet hoped it would never come.

The airman spoke up. "We surrender. We have no choice."

"That is good for you," Matelot said. "You'll be taken to a POW camp. Our fates will be less kind. We cannot afford to be tortured. Better that we all die than expose the rest of our cell."

"You would have us all killed?"

"If it protects the others, yes. I'm sorry. Surrender is not an option."

"We are waiting," the disembodied voice came again. "You have five minutes, and then we come in. If we have to do that, we will take no prisoners."

"Vogel," Matelot said grimly. "I recognise that bastard's voice from the print shop raid last month."

"Yes," said Renard. "I recognise it, too." He sighed and looked across at Matelot. "We are done for, Jacques. I don't see any way out of this."

Matelot nodded. "I know, Henri."

Matelot turned to Vigneron. "I love you, Simone. I had hoped for more." He paused. There was no need to finish the sentence, so he left it unspoken. "But if we die here, now, then I have had more than many men."

He kissed her lightly on the cheek.

"We die well, yes?"

She nodded and gripped the stock of her Sten gun, feeling the weight in her hands. "I know. But we die for France."

"What are you going to do?" one of the airmen asked.

"Group Captain, you stay here. When the Boche come in, surrender. They will not harm you. Just stay put."

He turned to the other two. "Ready?"

The Henri and Simone nodded. Both looked pale and frightened, and he suspected he probably looked terrified to them. He tightened his grip on the Sten and paused. Then:

"Let's go."

They walked to the door, hesitated briefly, then Matelot pushed it open and they ran out into the street, spraying it with machine-gun fire. While they died in a hail of bullets, they took several Wehrmacht soldiers with them. They fell back, thrown by the force of the rounds that tore through their bodies, to lie motionless in the street like rag dolls, blood pooling across the cobblestones.

When the gunfire ceased, SS-Untersturmführer Vogel stepped from one of the trucks and studied the bodies, turning them one at a time with the toe of his boot to make sure. He turned to one of the Wehrmacht soldiers.

"Go inside and round up the Allied airmen. They are prisoners of war, so treat them accordingly."

The man saluted. "Herr Untersturmführer."

Vogel turned to Unterscharführer Werner Schäfer.

"A pity. It would have helped to take them alive, Herr Unterscharführer. Dead men tell us nothing. Alive, we might have gained something."

"I'm not sure they were prepared to be taken alive, Herr Untersturmführer."

"No, indeed not." He sighed. "Still, a small victory, if not the one I had hoped for. Arrange for someone to clean up the mess."

"Yes, Herr Untersturmführer."

***

"Is there more of this?" Pascale said, her eyes flicking over the document.

"Yes, some names of agents. She mentions Jean-Luc, Mistral. Also, there is Anton Marchand, Orage, André Fournier, and the owner of the café, he's Aigle, Marguerite Fournier. It's not clear, but Fournier's wife, maybe? She is called Églantine in the journal. They blew up the railway. Here, look. Malaunay."

***

'Aigle set the charges at the viaduct before dawn. The train was due at first light. Mistral kept watch on the eastern approach. I watched the west.

The first explosion derailed the engine. It fell into the ravine, dragging coaches and men with it. The second tore through the carriages. Fire spread fast. Good. Plenty of Bosche killed.

Some Bosche fell on the tracks. Some didn't get up. We shot at those who did. Exchange of fire. We then disappeared into the trees.

By noon, we were scattered. Mistral didn't make the rendezvous. I waited an hour, then left.

Later, news came through—dozens dead, transport halted for days. They are hunting us now. Something wrong. Not sure what. Not an ammunition train. Poor intel?'

***

"The Germans carried out reprisals. Look."

***

'They came at dawn the following day. Trucks rolled into Mauraval. SS-Sicherheitsdienst poured out. Doors kicked in. People dragged into the street. Richter and Vogel in charge.

Ten people shot against the wall. A woman and her child among them. The mayor hanged from a lamppost.

Fires burned through the morning. Smoke visible for miles.

Our fault. We did this. I tell myself it was necessary but hate myself. The others say the same. Physically sick.

Mistral arrived eventually. Had to avoid patrols.

We move again tonight.'

***

Pascale sank her head in her hands. "Good God!"

Patrice placed an arm on her shoulder. "I know. We can only imagine what was going on in their minds. It was a dirty business. Maybe we would do the same in their place."

"I know, but…"

"Let me keep going through this. See if you can find anything on Vanguard."

Patrice sighed. "There must be more of this journal. Where is the rest, I wonder?"

They asked one of the archivists, but the only answer they got was a shrug. "*Désolé, monsieur*, that this was all there was. Copies of relevant entries. No one knows where the original document is."

As Pascale was deep in the stacks of papers, her phone buzzed. Expecting it to be Radfield or Clarice, she picked it up and frowned, seeing a withheld number. She hesitated before picking up the call.

"*Âllo?*"

"Pascale Hervé?" a voice on the other end said. The voice was low and masculine, and she could hear menace in the tone. "Listen carefully, and don't ask questions."

"Who is this?" she said, glancing across at Patrice, who was still hunched over a stack of documents, oblivious to the call. Her fingers tightened around the phone as she maintained her composure, keeping her voice calm.

"You're looking into Claire Lemoine's past, right?"

"What is that to you?"

"You're digging into dangerous territory. Leave well alone. Stop this investigation now, and no one will get hurt."

Pascale's heart skipped a beat, and she glanced again at Patrice, who was now looking up with a question written on his face. She put the phone on loudspeaker and shook her head. He nodded and remained silent.

"No one will get hurt? What about Monsieur Defrense? Like that?"

"Regrettable, madame. However, there are things better left undisturbed. You may find Madame Lemoine's details in the archives, but there are redactions for a reason. Some truths are not meant to be uncovered. You have no idea who you're involving yourself with. Back off. You don't want to get any deeper into this."

The voice paused as if waiting for her to respond, but Pascale remained silent. She felt her heart racing.

We are close to something. They are ruffled.

She took a breath before responding.

"Why should I listen to you?" she asked, her tone firmer now, hiding the uncertainty clouding her thoughts.

She heard a slight chuckle from the caller. "Because the past has a way of catching up with people. Claire Lemoine's story isn't just about the Resistance. There's more. Don't say I didn't warn you."

The line went dead.

Pascale sat frozen, looking at the phone on the table. Her mind spun with the implications. Was that someone from the Resistance who knew Claire? What truth were they trying to keep buried? She looked over at Patrice.

"Who was that?" he said, a curious look crossing his face.

Pascale shook her head. "Withheld number, so I have no idea, but we are treading on someone's toes. Radfield, Defrense, now this."

Her mind raced. She knew she couldn't ignore the warning, but she also felt more determined than ever to get to the bottom of Claire's story. She quickly shook her head, trying to regain focus.

"Warning me off has the opposite effect," she said.

"I had noticed. But we need to be careful."

The phone rang again.

"David," she said. She answered it. "*Âllo*, David."

"Pascale, how are you? I've just had a threatening phone call."

Patrice reached for his phone, which was buzzing in his pocket. He picked it up and answered. He gestured to Pascale. "That was Clarice..."

"Don't tell me, she's had a phone call."

They exchanged glances. "Time for a regroup," Pascale said. I think we need to talk to François as well."

***

Marseille, a few days later.

François Viala's office was small but cluttered. It was a mix of old, well-worn furniture and teetering piles of paperwork, many of which still remained from his predecessor, Commandant Carbonneau, and the modern desktop computer made it feel as if it was caught between different decades. Out in the main office, the fluorescent light continued to flicker as it had before Carbonneau killed himself following his exposure in a corruption scandal. A scandal from which the local police force was still recovering.

Capitaine François Viala sat behind the metal desk that didn't seem to quite fit him, and he made a mental note yet again to arrange for a replacement along with the other reminders of Carbonneau. He scanned the people sitting opposite him. His hands rested firmly on the edge of the desk. His posture was straight and slightly stiff, yet he was calm and focused. This was his domain now. Perhaps, not too far off, a rank to fit the office would be nice. The thought of a nameplate on the door announcing Commandant Viala had a ring to it..

Around the table sat Pascale, Patrice, Radfield, and Clarice, each trying to suppress their underlying fear while being keenly aware of the stakes. They looked at Viala, who appeared unaffected by the weight of the situation; however, the group knew that his calm demeanour was a mask, concealing the same uncertainty they felt beneath it.

"How far have you got with your investigation into Defrense's death?" Pascale said. "We've made some progress on the historical research in London and Paris, but we need to be careful. The more we uncover about *Grand-mère's* wartime activities, the more dangerous it becomes. Someone doesn't want this to come out. We've had one attempted assassination, and all of us have been warned off."

Viala nodded but remained silent for a moment as he considered her point. He glanced at the file on the desk in front of him, Defrense's photograph clipped to the inside, before looking back at Pascale. He met her gaze for a fraction of a second, and something unspoken passed between them, a recognition of shared danger. "I'm handling the investigation, but so far, we have nothing to go on. The cause of death was a heart attack. The pathologist said that it would have happened at any time, 'a heart attack waiting to happen,' were his exact words. However, there are subtle clues that someone was there. The bruises on the chest were post-mortem but fit with an attempt at resuscitation. So why try to save the man but not call for an ambulance? There is a mystery here that I need to unravel, although my commandant is unhappy about spending resources chasing a well-meaning phantom," he said. "Where have you got to with your research?"

"From what I have deduced, Claire Lemoine was working as a languages teacher near Leatherhead in Surrey," Radfield said. "Sometime after that, she turned up at SOE. I managed to find some records from there, but the attempt on our lives disrupted us somewhat. We were still in Leatherhead when I received the phone call warning me off."

"Well," Patrice said, "as an SOE operative, she ran an agent while she was in France. Most of her activities involved resistance work, including an escape line to Spain, but I found evidence of another agent. All I could find was a code name 'Vanguard', but the records suggest that she was Vanguard's go-between to SOE."

"Very good," Viala said. "So far, you have made some progress, while my investigation appears to have stagnated. Let's stay focused on our respective roles and share what we need to as we go. We can't afford to make mistakes."

There was a pause as they each processed what he'd said. Patrice shifted uneasily in his seat. "And what if those roles intersect? What if what we find about the past is tied to the present in ways we don't yet understand? The evidence is beginning to look that way. Why warn us off? Why did someone go to Defrense and cause his death? If that is what happened? Something that was a threat back then is a threat to someone today. I suggest we try to find out if anyone from that time is still alive."

Viala's jaw tightened slightly. "Then we deal with it. But we do it carefully. If someone's targeting you, we must stay smart and safe. Don't push too hard without backup. Keep me informed at all times, eh?"

Clarice looked around at the group, then at Viala. "So, we wait for you to act on the present and keep digging. But we share the findings when it's necessary?"

"Exactly," Viala said. "We all have the same goal here. To find the truth. However, we need to be mindful of the risks. Please, all of you, take care."

The silence that followed hung heavy with the weight of his words. Outside the office, they could hear seagulls wheeling and squabbling, but inside, everything felt suspended and time appeared slowed by the realisation that the truth they were chasing might be too dangerous to survive unscathed.

Pascale finally broke the stillness, her voice quieter now but determined. "Then let's move forward. But we stay cautious. We can't afford to trust anyone fully. Not yet."

Radfield took off his glasses and polished them as he tended to when thinking aloud. "I need to go back to Kew and pin down that Vanguard fellow. Now that I have a code name, I might find something. His real identity would be nice. I think, though," he looked at Clarice, "I will leave your mother behind on this occasion."

"She won't like it," Clarice said. "You know what she is like."

"I know, but I won't forgive myself if anything happens to her."

"She won't forgive you if anything happens to you, so please take care."

He smiled. "I will."

With that, they rose from the table, exchanging a glance that was both an unspoken agreement and a quiet acknowledgement that this fragile alliance between past and present, between detective and researcher, would be their only chance to uncover the truth about Claire Lemoine's activities in Nazi-occupied France. They left the office and walked out into the harsh sunlight, the weight of the investigation pressing down on their shoulders, knowing the real danger was only beginning.

Chapter 6

The Road to Pau

These roads were designed for the Indian FTR, Pascale thought. Taking care not to get caught by any of the grey speed cameras at the roadside and looking well ahead for any *flics* who might have set a mobile trap, she let the 1200cc Vee twin have its head and held on as the torque surged the machine forward at highly illegal speeds. Once off the Autoroute, she made the most of its agile handling through the twisty mountain roads in the foothills of the Pyrenees.

Clarice had been busy while she and Patrice were in Paris. "I have something," she said. "There is someone you might want to speak to."

"*D'accord?*"

"Dr. Étienne Caron. He is a local historian based in Pau. I discovered a paper he had written about a mysterious disappearance during the war. Around 1944, apparently. That's our timeline, is it not?"

Pascale stood and walked across to see Clarice's screen. "Yes, it is. What has he found?"

"According to this, there were some remains found a month back. A massacre..."

Pascale nodded. "I seem to remember something about that on the news a few weeks ago." She looked across at Patrice. "If you go back to Paris and see if you can find anything about Vanguard, I'll go to Pau and see what Dr Caron says."

The warm wind on her face was a release from the day-to-day as she accelerated, throttled off, braked and leaned the bike before twisting the throttle and hurtling up to speed on the straights before braking for the next bend. This bike, she thought, was made for these roads.

***

Dr Étienne Caron's house, nestled against the foothills of the Pyrenees on the outskirts of Pau. It was a modest stone cottage set back from the road in a well-tended garden. The limestone exterior was weathered with age, with ivy creeping along the walls and a somewhat haphazard slate roof with some tiles slipping. A narrow gravel path with lavender and rosemary in the beds alongside it led to a sturdy oak door.

Pascale parked the Indian, hooked her helmet over one of the mirrors, and unbuttoned her jacket. Placing her gloves in the messenger bag attached to the frame, she ran a hand through her hair before walking along the path to the cottage. She lifted the black iron door knocker and rapped it several times before hearing someone moving inside.

"I am coming. No need to knock the door down."

"*Désolé*," she said as he opened the door.

The sharp tone was a contradiction to the man who opened the door. Dr Étienne Caron was a kindly looking man of indeterminate years.

Like Radfield, she thought.

His face was lined with age, and his hair, streaked with silver, had receded to the edges of his scalp, leaving a narrow band above his ears that bushed out in wild abandon, as if in defiance of the loss of the rest of it to the passage of time. His eyes, with heavy bags hanging under them, were a deep brown and glinted with a hint of unspoken amusement.

Pascale held out a hand and introduced herself. "Dr Caron, you were expecting me?"

"Of course, my dear. Please, come in. Please excuse the mess, but an old man living alone cares little for tidiness these days."

"Your garden says otherwise, doctor."

"Ah, yes, a passion. That and the past, of course. Which is why you are here, is it not? Come on in, please."

She followed him to his study.

"Coffee, madame?"

"Yes, thank you." While she waited for him to fiddle with the coffee machine, she looked around the room. It was filled with books. They were everywhere: piled on tables, stacked against walls, and crammed into every available shelf and hidden beneath another pile, she could see an upright piano struggling for life. The air smelled faintly of old paper, wood smoke from the wood burner in the corner of the room, and freshly brewed coffee. A large desk sat by the window overlooking the distant peaks. As with every other available surface, this desk was covered in books, papers, historical documents, and faded photographs. The wood burner glowed bright orange and threw heat into the room, contrasting with the chill of the mountain air outside.

"So, Pascale said, sipping the hot coffee, what did you discover?"

"Ah," Caron sat down in his easy chair that seemed to swallow him up. "This period has always been a passion of mine. The route through the nearby mountains was one that the resistance used to reach Spain with allied airmen escaping the Bosche.

"There were stories that a group had died here. They were just that, it seemed, but I spent the summer about five years ago searching through the records and working out the exact routes they used. It's been a long search, but last month I was rewarded. The bodies were in a cave behind a rockfall, so unless anyone was looking, it is likely they would never have been found."

"How do you know this, Dr Caron?"

He smiled, and his face creased, almost hiding his eyes. "Because, my dear, I was the one who found them."

"How? How did you know where to look?"

He shrugged. "Landslides occur in the mountains. I was walking one of the routes used by the resistance and was looking for places they might have used to rest. Some of the rocks had moved and fallen away, exposing an opening. I would like to say it was a stroke of genius, but it was really nothing more than curiosity and luck. As I was following the trail and saw the opening in the rocks, so I looked inside, and there they were. Three skeletons. We eventually identified them using the documents we found on the bodies and dental records from before the war."

"Where is this, then?"

Caron put his cup down on the low table next to his chair. "Would you like to have a look?"

"Of course."

"Wait here." Caron went through the door into another room, and she could hear him rummaging about as he talked to himself. He reappeared a few moments later carrying a cagoule, woolly hat and walking boots. "You will need these in the mountains. Your motorcycle clothing is not adequate at all, madame."

"Yes, doctor. Thank you."

Pascale followed him out the back of the house to a tumbledown garage. He opened the doors and pulled a dust cover off an ancient Citroën 2CV.

"Get in."

Pascale clambered into the car alongside Caron, who grinned as he started the beast, and it fired into life at the first turn of the key. The car lurched as he forced the gear lever into first gear with a crunch, and they shot off at a speed that made Pascale smile. She recalled Radfield gripping the edge of the seat, his knuckles white when she drove him anywhere. Caron's driving would give the man nightmares for the rest of his life. Pascale was more than happy to live dangerously. The tight bends at breakneck speed made her grin as she glanced across to the driver gripping the wheel as if his life depended on it, while leaning forward to peer through his glasses at the road ahead, making adjustments as they reached a hazard rather than well in advance. This was a hold-onto-your-hat ride, and Pascale enjoyed every moment. Much like a fairground ride, but more dangerous and free.

Eventually, Caron brought the car to a juddering halt and wrenched the handbrake with a loud graunch.

"From here we walk, madame," he said.

The wind moaned through the mountains as Pascale followed Dr. Étienne Caron along the narrow path.

"The Spanish border is about five kilometres this way," he said.

"D'accord." Pascale paid close attention to where she was putting her feet as one missed step could involve a drop of several hundred metres down a sheer rock face.

The morning mist clung to the mountain peaks. High above, a solitary golden eagle circled, searching for prey. Occasionally, its cries echoed across the desolate sky.

Caron adjusted his scarf and glanced at her. "You're lucky, you know. Few people get to see this."

Pascale kept her hands tucked into her coat pockets. "A cave that was once full of bones?"

"An archaeological site," he said with a smile. "One that could change everything we know about the resistance in this region." He slowed his pace, gesturing ahead. "There."

A barrier had been placed before the entrance to the cave, and Caron pulled it aside and invited her to step past it. The cave entrance yawned open before them, half-hidden by a tumble of boulders and overgrown brush. Inside, the air was cool, damp. Pascale's boots crunched against loose stone as she stepped inside, eyes adjusting to the dim light. The scent of earth and decay lingered in the dank air.

Caron crouched beside some items. A leather holster and a beret. Some corroded cartridges from a magazine, carefully uncovered but still partly entwined with soil and debris. "I found them last month," he said. "Clearly a resistance cell." He paused and looked about at the items. "We are still collecting and bagging, so this is a work in progress. We don't know what happened. We are still trying to find that out. There is still evidence to uncover, as you can see, it is a work in progress."

"Then we are looking to solve the same puzzle," Pascale said. "And where are the remains now? Have they been buried?"

Caron shook his head. They are still with the pathologist. I can take you there if you have seen enough here?"

"D'accord."

They made their way back down the track to the car. Caron drove them to the Institut de Pathologie in Pau.

Caron led her into the building, walking briskly along the corridors until he reached a door and knocked.

"Come in."

He opened the door. "Ah, Dr Renaud."

Dr Raphael Renaud stood. "Dr Caron, what a pleasant surprise, what brings you here?"

Caron held out a hand. "This is Pascale Hervé, she is researching the same people we found in the caves. At least, we suspect that is the case."

"Ah, madame, *enchanté*. Please, follow me."

Renaud led them to his lab, where the bodies were kept in their drawers. Renaud pulled them out. He walked to each body in turn and identified it.

Caron reached for a clipboard that he had secreted in his messenger bag. "We've managed to identify them. Although the documents they carried were false, dental records helped us."

He turned a page, ran a finger down a list of names, and met Pascale's gaze.

"One of them was Jean-Luc Defrense." He let the name settle between them. "Codename Mistral. Does that name mean anything to you, madame?"

Pascale's pulse quickened. "So, it is them. Yes, that is one of the cell members we are trying to trace. And Claire Lemoine?"

He shook his head. "No, these are all men." He looked back at the clipboard. Anton Marchand, codename Orage and André Fournier, code name Aigle."

"There is something else, madame," Renaud said. "This one, Defrense, did not die naturally. Here," he pointed at the skull. In the middle of the forehead was a hole. "A bullet. Close range. Executed. For the others, the cause of death was also shooting, but to the torso. As you can see, there is damage to the ribs caused by the bullets."

Caron stood back and held the clipboard close to his chest. "Does this help with your search, madame?"

"In part. From what we discovered at the *Archives Nationales*, Marchand was a messenger for the group. He was also involved in acts of sabotage. They derailed a troop train in 1943, and the records suggest that he was the one who laid the charges. Fournier was previously in the army before the fall of France, like Defrense. Again, we found records relating to him. His main job was reconnaissance, and he would guide airmen out of France. But," she paused, "it doesn't help with what happened to Claire Lemoine. She vanished at the same time as these three. And you found no signs of any other bodies?"

"No," Caron straightened, brushing imaginary dust from his coat. "In that, madame, I cannot help. There is nothing here that suggests she was with these men."

"Or that she wasn't."

"Indeed, or that she wasn't."

She paused and looked back at the remains. "Have you identified any living relatives of these men? Defrense, we already know about and he is now dead. If there is anyone else we can track down, it would be useful."

Caron shook his head. "The police have been working on that, but nothing so far. We do know that Fournier had a son, but as yet, they have not traced him. That is for them, rather than I, madame."

Pascale nodded. "Of course, monsieur. I understand. However, if you do discover anything, it might help."

Pascale exhaled, staring at the bones. The past had been buried here for decades. And now she had to make sense of it. Who had shot Jean-Luc Defrense, and what happened to Claire and Vanguard?

Pierrefitte-sur-Seine, Present day

Patrice again sat at a table, surrounded by brittle and faded photographs. This time, he had one focus. He was tracking down references to Vanguard. Any hint of who this man was would help. All he found on the previous visit was a vague reference in Claire Lemoine's journal.

His phone buzzed, and he glanced at it. He smiled and picked up.

"David. How is England?"

"Wet. How are things in Paris?"

"Same here. Plenty of papers to work through. I am still looking for further information on Vanguard." He could almost hear the smile at the other end.

"Well, Patrice, I have a lead. I've found an SOE file. Confirmation of recruitment and service details. It's heavily redacted, but I have a name and date of birth."

Patrice stiffened. "Go on."

"He was deployed to France in October 1941. The mission details are redacted or missing. He was managed and trained by a man called Arthur Spencer. Vanguard was a chap called James Kerr, born April 15th, 1913. Fluent in French and German, so a shoo-in for Intelligence. I'm going to start searching census records for Scotland. See if we can get a bit more family background."

"Scotland?"

"Aye, our laddie was a Scot. He was born in Crieff."

Patrice thought about this for a moment. "He would have been in his late twenties by the time the war broke out. I wonder if he was already part of British intelligence or if they recruited him later."

"Much of this has been redacted, but given he was a German speaker, they would have targeted him as they did with Claire Lemoine."

"Keep at it, David. See what you can find."

"If they were still in Scotland when he was young, they'll be on the census."

Patrice was silent for a moment. "And if they weren't, David?"

"Then we look elsewhere." He could hear Radfield shuffling through the file again. "But we've got something solid now. I'll update you when I get to Edinburgh."

"Good. Keep at it. In the meantime, have you had any problems?"

"Not so far, but I'm keeping an eye out for trouble."

"Take care."

***

Kew, Present Day.

Radfield hung up and put the phone down. He continued leafing through the information, but it told him little else he could use. He put everything back and texted Pascale and Patrice.

"All done here for the moment. Might return if needed, but off to Edinburgh to follow the lead on James Kerr, aka Vanguard."

He then booked a rail ticket for the following morning to Edinburgh Waverley.

***

National Records of Scotland, Edinburgh, Present Day.

Radfield introduced himself at the desk and waited until an employee came to show him to the records department.

"Come this way, Mr Radfield." Radfield looked at her name tag, Jennifer McLeish.

"Thank you, Jennifer."

Radfield followed her to the dimly lit reading room. He could smell the aroma of aged paper, hear the quiet movement of pages turning, and the hushed conversations surrounding him. The clerk at the front desk barely looked up as he approached with Jennifer.

"How may I help?"

"I need access to the 1921 census records," Redfield said, slipping a note with the name James Kerr and the date of birth, April 1915.

The clerk adjusted his glasses and took the slip. "You'll find census microfilms in the research room. Birth records are separate—we only have official copies."

"That will be fine for my needs." Radfield thanked him and moved deeper into the archives. Minutes later, he inserted a reel into the microfilm reader, scanning through lists of names. The flickering light from the screen reflected in his glasses as he focused.

Then, he found it.

Kerr, James Joseph. Age: 8. Born: 1913. Residence: Crieff.

His mother's name followed. His mother, Hannah Kerr, nee Krüger, was German, and his father, Malcolm Kerr, was a railway engineer. The address was a small house in Crieff.

Radfield leaned back. "Well, now, that is interesting. A Scottish father. A German mother. Very interesting indeed. It puts a whole new perspective on matters. No wonder he was of interest to Arthur Spencer and his outfit."

Fishing his phone out of his pocket, he called Patrice.

"Patrice, I have him," he said. "Vanguard was born James Joseph Kerr, born in Crieff in 1913, as his SOE records already tell us. His father wasn't listed at the house in 1921, so I did more digging. He served in the Royal Scots during World War I. He was listed as missing in action and presumed dead. So James was brought up by his mother. But what is interesting is that he was half-German. I'll dig deeper while I'm here."

Patrice exhaled. "Good work, David. Keep me updated."

Radfield hung up and turned back to the records. If Vanguard had been in the Special Operations Executive, there would be more—maybe in old military files or war records.

And if the war had buried him, Radfield would ensure he was found.

Radfield scrolled through the census records again, his eyes scanning the details. James Kerr was listed in the 1921 Scottish census, but by 1931, he was gone. There was no record of him in Crieff, and his mother was not at the same address.

"They must have moved. I wonder where?"

He sat for a moment, drumming his fingers on the desk. The old Detective Inspector Radfield was getting to work in his mind, following clues and seeking those hidden below the surface. He smiled to himself and went back to the main desk.

"Excuse me, but do you have any information regarding emigration?"

"Of course. If you give me a moment. I'll bring the fiche over to you."

Once again, with the microfiche in place, he started scanning. Then, he found what he was looking for. "Once an old detective, always an old detective." His hunch had paid off.

He picked up the phone. "Patrice."

"Yes?"

"I have another lead. I will be travelling to Berlin."

"Oh?"

"It looks as if the family went there shortly after the 1921 census. I will arrange travel and get back to you."

***

It was still raining when Radfield stepped outside and returned to the hotel. He turned up his collar and pulled his Panama hat low over his face. As he walked, he sensed rather than saw the tail.

He kept walking steadily, resisting the urge to look over his shoulder. He didn't want the tail to realise he had been spotted. The streets were slick from the evening rain, with the glow of streetlights reflecting off wet cobblestones. He caught a glimpse in a shop window. Still there. A figure, a few paces behind, always just far enough to avoid suspicion. He was not a random pedestrian.

He crossed the road without hesitation, weaving between slow-moving cars. He confirmed it in the glass of a parked bus shelter. He watched the reflection—his tail crossed, too.

Sod it!

Reaching a narrow close, he stepped inside, pressing his back against the damp stone wall. The light from the streetlamp didn't reach this far, and the shadows swallowed him. He listened. Footsteps approached, steady and deliberate. Then they slowed and stopped.

Radfield waited until the moment passed. The figure hesitated at the entrance, scanning the alley, then moved on. Radfield moved. A service door to his right. It was unlocked.

Bit of luck.

He opened it and slipped inside, closing it quietly behind him.

Through the dim interior of what seemed to be a pub's storage room, he found another exit leading up to the bar. He ascended the stairs and walked into the bar. It was getting busy, and no one paid him any attention. He moved through the crowd and out of the main entrance, which opened onto a different street. He stepped out, walking calmly toward his hotel. The tail wouldn't see him now. But someone had been watching.

The buggers mean business.

Once in his room, he closed the door behind him, locking it out of habit. He exhaled slowly, rubbing a hand over his face. He removed his damp coat and hung it up, placing his fedora on the hook by the door. His pulse was still steady but elevated, and his heart was still beating faster than it should. He crossed to the window, pulling the curtain back just enough to check the street below. No sign of his tail. But that didn't mean he was alone.

The landline phone rang. He looked at it. He let it ring twice, then picked it up. There was a pause. Then a voice. No accent he could place.

"Walk away, Chief Inspector."

He could hear static on the line. He said nothing, waiting.

"Chief Inspector, we warned you. Back off. This is your last warning."

Still, he remained silent. *Let him speak.*

"You don't want to be in Edinburgh tomorrow." Click. The line went dead.

Radfield sighed and replaced the receiver. His hand lingered on it for a moment. Then he turned back to the window. This wasn't over.

Bugger.

He smiled to himself. He was leaving Edinburgh. That much was certain.

Chapter 7

Frankfurt, 1936

The rain came in fine sheets on a light, bitter easterly. The mourners stood by the graveside, clutching umbrellas as they listened to the priest's final words for an old friend. James Kerr stood by the graveside in a black coat and fedora hat, watching silently, his jaw tightening as he stared at the coffin. He became aware of someone coming up next to him. He turned slightly. Emil Brecht's bulky frame loomed beside him and shook his umbrella slightly, a cold edge to his voice as he spoke. "A good man, Otto," he said, adjusting his homburg.

"Yes. I owe him much. And you?"

"He was my mentor at the *Kulturverein*. We served together on the staff in Berlin during the war before that."

Kerr nodded. He lapsed into silence as they lowered the coffin into the ground and the incantation of everlasting life carried across the damp air.

"I am correct in thinking that you will be taking over Otto's work?"

Brecht nodded. "The world may be changing, but there is still much to be done. Otto would want that."

"Of course."

"And you, Herr Krüger?" Brecht asked, his tone measured. "I trust the name, your mother's, has served you well here?"

Kerr's lips pressed into a thin line, a flicker of memory crossing his face. Hanna's frail hands, her German lullabies, the name Krüger she'd given up in a hostile land. "It has," he said quietly. "It's kept me safe." He paused, looking at the other mourners and the priest reading from his bible, his words a familiar drone. "Yes. The world is changing, Herr Brecht. I have to do my duty, you understand?"

"Of course. Every man must attend to his duty, Herr Krüger."

James nodded. "Then you will understand. I have to go back to Scotland now."

Bercht hesitated and turned to face him. "I see. And then?"

"I have arranged to take a commission in the Royal Scots. My father's regiment. Europe is becoming a more dangerous place."

Brecht nodded. "Of course." He smiled and held out a gloved hand, and Kerr took it. *"Alles klar."*

Kerr's hand brushed the cigarette case in his pocket, the "A.K." engraving a silent reminder of Otto's words. *Alles klar*, ready for what's next.

***

Café Lys Noir, Rouen, Autumn 1941

André Fournier leaned against the bar, wiping a glass with a rag that had seen better days. The Café Lys Noir was quiet, the morning sun filtering through shuttered windows. The lunchtime crowd would come in later. His wife, Marguerite, polished glasses beside him, her movements brisk but silent. Occasionally, she would catch his eye and smile. After all these years, he thought, there is still a spark. A little light in the darkness that hung over France. A small hope for the future.

A Verdun veteran, André still experienced the flashbacks, and a sudden noise, such as a car backfire or a dropped crate, would cause him to jolt and leave him visibly shaken before he could regain his composure. His loathing for the Germans had simmered ever since the trenches. However, since the fall of France and the flood of grey uniforms of the occupying forces now using his café, he kept a neutral smile for the Wehrmacht soldiers and Gestapo officers who would soon fill the place, but that neutral smile and jovial 'bonjour' hid a determination to undermine them wherever he could. Killing as many as he could became a burning obsession.

The door swung open, and Anton Marchand strode in, his bicycle shop apron swapped for a worn jacket, his flat cap firmly on his head and his chin unshaven as was usual during the week. Anton shaved for God on a Sunday. Everyone else made do with the coal tar chin. Likewise, the grubby cap. André wondered if he ever took it off to sleep.

"Are the others here?" he said.

"Upstairs. You're the last. I'll be up soon."

Anton nodded, his boots clumping up the wooden stairs. André's gaze lingered on the staircase, his thoughts on the meeting ahead.

"Papa?" Their ten-year-old son, Jacques, emerged from the back. "Why is Uncle Anton here with all those people?"

André ruffled the boy's hair, forcing a smile. "Adult business, Jacques. Stay with Maman. You'll see Anton later, d'accord?"

The boy pouted but climbed onto a stool, watching Marguerite as she quietly prepared the café for the evening's business. "Go on, André," she said. "You can fill me in on the meeting later."

André climbed the stairs to the cramped upstairs room. Around the table, familiar faces watched him. Anton, Pierre, with his thick glasses, Suzanne, his young wife, and the Dufresne brothers, Jean-Luc and Henri, Jacques Morel and Simone. Ordinary French people drawn into extraordinary circumstances.

Anton Marchand, ex-army signaller and now a bicycle shop owner; Suzanne Moreau, his young receptionist; her husband Pierre, a former forger; Jean-Luc Dufresne, a jobless taxi driver whose taxi had been impounded by the occupying forces; his brother Henri, a quiet motor mechanic, demobbed when France was defeated the previous year; Jacques Morel, a burly dock worker from Le Havre; and Simone Berthier, his fiancée, clutching a scarf.

André looked at all of them, one at a time, as his eyes swept the room. They all seemed unremarkable, yet they were about to become a part of something bigger than themselves.

"What did London say?" André asked, settling into a chair.

Anton looked around the group. "They're sending someone. Codename Flamme. The drop details are to follow. I'll go and meet her once I have the details. But there's more. They say there's an operative here already. Code name Vanguard."

André frowned, his fingers tightening on the table. "Vanguard? Why haven't we heard from him?"

"Establishing his cover, London says," Anton said flatly. "Flamme will be his contact."

Jean-Luc shifted uneasily. "How do we know this Vanguard's not a Boche plant?"

The room was quiet. Anton frowned. "According to London, he parachuted in a few weeks ago. So he has come from SOE. I am not worried on that score. Flamme will be his link to London, so we won't deal directly with him. That's all the information I have on the matter."

There were nods around the room, and Jean-Luc's qualms were dismissed.

"For now," André said, "we wait for Flamme."

***

England, Winter 1941

The night was cold and moonless. Claire Lemoine looked up. A smuggler's moon, clouds drifting low over the runway, and frost covering the ground. Perfect conditions. A Westland Lysander sat on the tarmac, its black fuselage barely distinguishable against the darkness. The ground crew worked with hushed efficiency, fuelling the aircraft while the pilot performed preflight checks.

Arthur Spencer stood with his hands in his pockets. As Claire looked across at him, his breath hung in clouds in the cold air. This was it. The culmination of nearly six months of training since she agreed to join SOE. After two weeks of initial vetting and assessment at Wanborough Manor, she travelled to Scotland for her paramilitary training, then back south to Manchester for parachute training. Finally, she went to Beaulieu for espionage training. Now, finally, here, deployment in the field. She gulped down the lump in her throat. Preparation was one thing, but this was reality, and she wondered if, despite the training, she was ready.

Spencer looked at her. "It's normal," he said. "Everyone feels afraid. You wouldn't be human if you didn't."

"Terrified would be a better word."

"Yes, I know."

He opened his cigarette case and offered one. She shook her head. He put one in his mouth and lit it, drawing deeply and tapping the ash onto the ground. "It won't be long now," he said as the Lysander coughed into life, sounding loud on the still air, and revved up to speed. The pilot taxied the plane out towards the runway.

Spencer turned to her. And handed her a final set of documents and a small cyanide pill hidden in a brass container.

"A member of the resistance cell will be at the landing site. He will take you to Rouen. Vanguard will contact you. Go to the Café Lys Noir in Rouen. The Patronne is one of ours. Code name Églantine. Once you have made contact with Vanguard, let us know. On no account are you to speak to anyone else about Vanguard. No one, clear? Any communication between you is strictly confidential, between you, him and me."

"Clear."

"If capture is imminent, you know what to do," he said, nodding at the brass pill box. His tone was firm but not unkind. "Better that than being taken by the Nazis."

She nodded and felt the pill box in her hand. She sighed. Hopefully, she would never have to use it.

While they stood breathing in the crisp air and shivering slightly, the pilot signalled that he would take off in five minutes. Spencer nodded and waved back.

"Better go, then," he said.

Claire adjusted her parachute harness, feeling its weight settle against her back. It was strange, she thought, how this seemed so natural in such a short space of time.

As she looked across at Spencer, she gulped again and hoped that her heart rate would return to normal. She was a language teacher, not an espionage agent. Or, she was. Now, she felt alien in her own skin. She was no longer the woman she once was. Never in the years she had grown up in rural France had she considered this a possibility; yet here she was on a cold, lonely airstrip in the middle of the night, waiting to join the war effort.

"Look after Colette," she said.

"Don't worry about her," Spencer said. "She will be in good hands, even if the worst happens."

She nodded. "I'll keep you to it."

"Of course. Don't worry about her. Concentrate on the mission and come back safe."

Spencer studied her for a long moment. "This is your last chance," he said. "If you have doubts, second thoughts. If you call it a day, no one will think any worse of you. You're absolutely sure?"

She took a deep breath. "I am," she said. "No going back."

He nodded. "Jolly good. I thought as much. Once you are on the ground, contact the resistance in Rouen. Églantine will put you in touch. The usual things, such as sabotage, establishing safe houses, and getting allied aircrew out of occupied France, take second place to anything Vanguard asks you to do. You report directly to him out there, right?"

"*D'accord.*"

He grinned at her lapse into French. "The Gestapo are pretty active, so keep your head down."

Spencer gripped her shoulder as the Lysander's engine revved up, ready to depart. "We'll be listening for you. As soon as you can, call Kingfisher on the radio."

Claire glanced back at the entrance of the airfield, where Spencer's car awaited. She took one last, deep breath before facing the unknown.

She ran across the grass to the tarmac and clambered into the rear cockpit of the aircraft.

"All set?" the pilot said.

"All set."

"Roger."

Spencer watched motionless as the Lysander taxied down the runway, gaining speed before ascending into the dark sky, its black shape disappearing into the night.

Claire sat in the rear cockpit, thinking about the jump and the first time she had done this, a mere few weeks before.

***

RAF Ringway, Manchester, 1941

The Armstrong Whitworth Whitley left the tarmac as dusk fell over RAF Ringway. Claire sat with the others in the aircraft's hull, trying to shut out the deafening noise and shaking of the airframe. She looked at her fellow trainees, who appeared as wan as she felt. Her stomach churned. Jumping in a hangar and landing from a platform was one thing, but never had she thought about launching herself into the air with nothing to prevent sudden death but a bundle of silk and cords no thicker than her bootlaces. Silk, they had been rigorously trained and checked to ensure that it was packed properly and would open when needed. They had packed their chutes themselves and unpacked them and repeatedly, under the critical eye of their instructor, a gruff forty-year-old Welshman, a paratroop sergeant major called Harry Williams. He accepted nothing less than perfection and would bark at anyone who fell short of the mark.

"That's your life there, in that piece of silk, Boyo, and you love it like it's your dear lady," he once said to a trainee who struggled with the task. "Go on, again, Boyo and keep doing it until you can do it in your sleep."

Sitting opposite her, looking obscenely comfortable, he grinned below his bushy moustache as he watched his charges about to make their first jump.

He's loving this, Claire thought, returning his gaze with a glower that seemed to widen the grin, showing even white teeth.

The noise was so loud she could barely think.

"Over the drop zone," the co-pilot said.

"Well, boys and girls," Williams said with undisguised relish. It's time to say cheerio." He opened the hatch and gestured for them to approach. When it was Claire's turn, she stood, clutching the cold metal of the bulkhead as the aircraft tilted to port, the open countryside below. The noise of the engines and the wind that whipped past, tearing at her body, increased the sense of dread that was now threatening to bring her simple meal eaten before leaving the aerodrome back up. She could taste the bile in her throat.

"Go on, my lovely, jump!"

She turned to look at him and shouted above the cacophony. "Is now a good time to tell you I don't like heights, Sergeant Major?"

He laughed and shoved her firmly into the small of her back. "You'll be fine, my lovely."

Then she was flying through the air. She could feel the wind tearing at her limbs, pushing the flesh of her face to the bone, the ground rushing up to meet her, her thoughts now clear. The training kicked in, and she pulled the release cord, and the parachute deployed, arresting her fall. As she drifted, she saw her fellows falling slowly to earth. There was a quiet calm after the noise of the aircraft. Looking up, she could see it disappearing in the evening sky, making its way back to base. Looking down, the ground seemed to rush up to meet her. She braced herself, and as she hit the ground, bent her knees, absorbed the impact and rolled.

She looked across the field as the others landed.

That wasn't so bad after all.

***

The memory faded, replaced by the steady hum of the Lysander's engine pulling them through the night sky. Claire sat in silence, hands wrapped around the straps of her harness, trying not to shiver. She wondered if it was the cold or the nerves as the aircraft flew southeast.

"We're approaching the drop zone," the pilot said.

"Roger."

She pushed back the canopy and felt the freezing air rush past her as she stood in the cockpit, ready to jump. Below, France stretched out, and she could see the fields of her home country.

This time, there was no shove on her back. No cheery Welsh voice *off you go, my lovely*. Just the mission ahead and the lives depending on her.

She adjusted her pack, glanced at the pilot, who nodded, and climbed and steadied herself, bracing against the bulkhead.

France was waiting. And she was ready.

"Off you go. *Bonne chance*," the pilot shouted, his words swept away by the wind.

Claire stepped out of the cockpit and jumped into the void.

***

The air remained icy, accompanied by a light easterly breeze. Above, the parachute billowed, slowing her descent. They had carefully chosen the night for the drop, and the moon was absent. The wind intensified, pushing her off course.

Merde!

She tugged at the risers, adjusting her trajectory, peering down into the darkness, hoping that she was now over the landing site.

The countryside was enveloped in a blanket of darkness. She sensed, rather than saw, the ground as it rushed up to meet her. She relaxed her legs, bent her knees, and rolled as she hit. She felt a sharp pain in her ankle. She reached down and rubbed it. It was nothing, she decided and stood up. Then, following her training, she started to pull the parachute in. Looking to the east, in the darkness, she could just about make out a tree line.

I am in the right place.

She wrenched off the harness, her breath coming in short gasps. She paused briefly to calm down and quell the fear. Having pulled the parachute into a bundle, she started dragging it toward the tree line. She could hear a dog bark in the distance.

Once she reached the trees, she unhitched the fold-up shovel on her belt and started to dig frantically. She scrambled the parachute into a round bundle, stuffing the silk into a hollow at the base of a tree, covering it with dirt and leaves. She stopped and cocked her head, listening to the night. The sound of an engine, slamming doors, boots and voices

Merde! The Bosche must have heard the plane!

As she stood frozen on the spot, she heard a low whistle. She smiled. The arranged signal. She turned and looked about. Her heart was still pounding. She slipped her pistol from her pocket, her finger resting along the barrel. She repeated the whistle. Then she heard a rustle in the undergrowth. A shadow moved between the trees.

"You must be Flamme," a voice said.

She looked around to see a man standing almost beside her. "Anton Marchand, sorry, Orage, I keep forgetting." He held out a hand. She shook it and returned to her task, covering the remains of the parachute, aided by Marchand.

"We had better hurry," he said. "The Bosche have heard the aircraft. They will be looking for you."

"I know. I heard them from the road."

"Quickly," he hissed, beckoning her forward. "They'll be here soon." He walked along the tree line to where two bicycles leaned against a tree, near the gate to the road. "Here," he handed her one, already straddling his own. As she straddled the machine, they saw headlights cutting through the trees and sweeping the fields. And voices in German shouting orders.

"Pedal. Now," Marchand said. They took off along a narrow dirt path from the main road through the woods. She pedalled, her legs burning as they pushed forward. Behind them, they could hear the sound of an engine and the voices of soldiers crashing through the trees. One of them let off a shot and was immediately rebuked.

They reached a crossroads at the edge of the woods just as a German patrol truck appeared on the main road.

"This way," Anton said, veering off to the left, following another narrow path back into the woods.

The truck slowed down, its searchlight sweeping the woods. They reached a downhill slope that took them deeper into the wooded area below the searchlights' line. Claire held her breath, gripping the handlebars tightly as they coasted downhill, out of sight.

Anton led them out of the woods onto the road further east of the crossroads. They looked back up the road and saw the vehicles standing and the soldiers moving about in the headlights, but the shadows concealed them this far down the hill.

"This way," Anton said. "Not too far."

They eventually reached a small farmhouse. Anton stopped and dismounted. He walked up to the door and knocked. The door opened, and a man ushered them in.

"Come on, get inside. Bring the cycles in as well. There are Bosche everywhere. Come on, come on!"

They didn't need further encouragement, so they pushed the bikes through the open door into the farmhouse kitchen, lit by a single candle, where the air smelled of damp wool combined with a general animal musk. A dog lay by the fireside, looked up with a low gruff, and returned to sleep.

The farmer looked at them both. "You had better go into the cellar in case the Bosche come looking."

"They will," Anton said. "They are searching along the road."

He took them along a short hallway and pulled a rug away from the floor. Beneath it was a trapdoor leading down to the cellar. They descended the stone steps as the farmer closed the trapdoor above them.

A few minutes later, they heard the sound of vehicles pulling up outside. Again, the noise of soldiers clambering out of the vehicles, their boots loud on the ground. There was a loud bang on the door.

"*Aufmachen! Aufmachen!*"

They heard the farmer shuffling across the floor and opening the door. Then they heard the sound of boots running through the house. Another voice asked if the farmer had heard or seen anything.

"*Merde!*" Anton said.

"What?" Claire said.

"Vogel. SS. Shh!"

They remained silent as the soldiers moved about the house, then left, and the door closed. The vehicle engines revved into life, and then they were gone. The farmer opened the trap door and called down to them.

"They have gone."

"We were lucky there," Anton said. "Welcome to the war, Flamme."

***

Frankfurt, 1931

James Kerr arrived home from school, pushing the door open, he caught the familiar smell of tobacco smoke and smiled as he hung his satchel on the hook in the hallway.

"Otto," he said, walking towards the front room.

Otto Reinhardt sat opposite Hanna, sipping a coffee. He placed the half-empty cup on the low table as James entered the room. "James, my boy, you are looking well. I thought I would drop in to see how you were progressing."

"Working hard, Otto," James said.

Hanna stood, smoothing her skirt. She gave a slight smile. "I'll leave you two to talk. Let me know if you want more coffee, Herr Reinhardt."

"Otto, please, Hanna. I feel we are friends by now."

She smiled and nodded. "Otto. I'll be in the kitchen if you want me."

Once alone, Otto pulled out his cigarette case and lit another cigarette. James looked down at the ashtray and deduced that Otto had been waiting for at least an hour before he arrived home from school. He sat on the sofa opposite Otto Reinhardt.

"What is it that brings you here, Otto?"

"Can I not look in on one of my charges?" He looked at James with a narrowed eye as he blew smoke into the room.

James grinned. "You always have a reason, Otto. There is always something."

Otto tapped off some ash and smiled. "You are as sharp as ever, boy. Yes, yes, there is something. I wondered what you were planning about university."

"Ah, yes. I wasn't sure." He frowned. Deciding at this stage, while essential, seemed so premature. He had his whole life ahead, yet adults, Otto in particular, were pushing him to make decisions that would affect his path before he felt fully ready.

Otto leaned back. "What do you like. I mean, what drives you? What makes you passionate? So passionate that you have to do it, no matter what?"

James gave this a moment's thought. "History."

"Good. Then study history. It will give you a fine degree. Something you can work with. Anything else?"

"My tutors feel that I should study English and French."

Otto narrowed his eyes again and smiled. "Again, good choices. Languages open so many doors in this modern world. Have you thought about which university you are going to apply to?"

James looked at him, momentarily feeling that he was being interrogated. "My history tutor suggested Leipzig," he said. "But why do I feel that you have already thought this through?"

"Because I have," Otto smiled. "Leipzig. An excellent choice. Yes, I approve. And when you leave university, any thoughts on that score?"

James shook his head. "No, not really. It's a long way off. Honestly, I'm more worried about finishing tomorrow's assignments, Otto. I have a lot of studying, I have little time to think about great plans for the future."

"Oh, it will be with you soon enough. Have you thought about the army?"

James inclined his head. "I hadn't given it much thought. But maybe. It's not something I would rule out. It might make a good career."

"It will make an excellent career choice, James. Trouble is brewing," Otto said. Mark my words. There is going to be another war. The army will be a good place to be. When the balloon goes up, a history professor isn't what the world needs, but a good army officer. A good army officer with a command of foreign languages will be a fine asset." He paused. "Officers who understand strategy, culture, languages and not just for the battlefield."

James frowned. "What do you mean by that?"

Otto shook his head and stubbed out the cigarette. "That is another discussion for another day. In the meantime, get that application in."

James nodded. "I will speak to my tutors about applying for Leipzig."

Otto stood. "Excellent, my boy." He put on his homburg, picked up his walking cane, and made for the door as he walked, he stumbled slightly and James caught his arm.

"Are you feeling unwell, Otto?"

"No, no," Otto shook his head. "Old age catching up with me, that is all. Nothing to worry about. Give my best to your mother."

***

Café Lys Noir, Rouen, Winter, 1941

The café was a dimly lit establishment in the back streets of Rouen, with faded paintwork and windows that hadn't seen a window cleaner for decades. It was frequented by resistance members, dockworkers, and German officers alike. It was a place where whispered conversations disappeared into the hum of daily life, where friend and foe rubbed shoulders in a neutral environment infused with the aroma of Gauloises, the sweet aniseed smell of Pernod and cooking mutton. The room was alive with quiet murmurs, the clink of glasses, and the occasional laughter from a Gestapo officer at the back table.

Outside, it was cold and damp. A fine drizzle fell from the sky and hung on Claire's hair and beret in tiny droplets. Rain slicked the cobbled streets outside, and at one point, she had to step away quickly as several German trucks roared past, spraying water up from the gutter. *Merde!*

Across the street, she saw a man in a dark coat and hat pulled low, concealing his eyes. He stopped and looked her way. She kept her eyes down and continued walking. *Gestapo.* He paused in a doorway and watched, but made no attempt to follow her. She was thankful to reach the café. She shook droplets from her coat as she pushed open the door and stepped inside, relishing the warmth after the chill outside. Her throat caught, and her eyes stung by the haze of smoke.

She walked across the floor, weaving deliberately but cautiously between the tables, taking in the German soldiers at one table and the Gestapo officer opposite. He laughed again at something one of his colleagues said and briefly caught her eye, but she looked away. Even the soldiers were keeping their distance. The other tables were occupied by locals who kept their heads down, focused on their quiet conversations and sipping their Pernod. She took off her gloves as she approached the counter, where Marguerite Fournier wiped a glass with a cloth and looked at her. A middle-aged woman with sharp eyes and a careful manner said nothing as she watched Claire walk toward her across the room. When Claire arrived at the counter, Marguerite put the glass down and poured a brandy, passing it across.

"You're late, *Cherié*," she said.

Claire placed her bag on the counter and drank the brandy, feeling the warmth course down her gullet. She put the empty glass back on the counter and leaned against it as she scanned the room again.

"Traffic," she said. "There were checkpoints. Someone is watching outside."

Marguerite nodded. "Yes. He's been there several nights now. We have to be careful." She slid a demitasse of espresso toward her. Then, as she refilled another customer's glass of wine, she placed a small, folded napkin beside Claire's cup. The movement was practised and seamless.

Claire picked it up, placed her coffee cup over it, held it in her hand, and walked to an empty table. There, she sat with the coffee, looking about the room. No one was paying any attention. Even the Gestapo officer was more interested in telling a tale to his companions. Again, there was loud laughter, but no one else was laughing, not even his companions. She unfolded the napkin and surreptitiously looked at it beneath the table. A single line was written inside in a neat hand.

"Upstairs. Alone."

There was no name, but she wouldn't have expected one.

She tucked the note into her sleeve, took a careful sip of the espresso, and let a few minutes pass before rising. She took another quick glance around the café. No sign of unusual attention, though the Gestapo officers at the back were watching the waitress a little too closely. She smiled to herself. Whatever was on their minds, it wasn't secrets. She walked past the counter, exchanging a brief glance with Marguerite before entering the passageway that led to the back of the building and the stairs at the rear leading to the first-floor rooms. She felt her heartbeat steady but quicken. She gulped. The stairs creaked underfoot, and she paused. No one came. The dimly lit corridor was narrow, and the floor uneven. A single lamp flickered at the end of the hall. She walked toward it. The door was slightly ajar. She hesitated for a fraction of a second, then stepped inside.

The room was dark, and she stood momentarily to allow her eyes to adjust. She could just about make out the window on the far wall, where a little of the light from outside came in, but with the blackout, that wasn't much. It was, however, enough to see a shadow of the figure waiting by the window, his hat pulled low.

She could make out the glow of a cigarette and smell the smoke as he drew on it. Outside, the rain had become heavier, and she could hear the patter as it splashed against the window, then the engines of another truck convoy splashing its way along the narrow road.

He didn't get up or even look her way. He was little more than a dark shape in the shadow.

"Flamme," he said. "You are late."

She tensed slightly. She hadn't expected him to speak English.

"Yes," she said. "Checkpoints. Vanguard?"

"Yes."

English, but with a very slight, almost imperceptible accent. A burr. She tried to place it. She saw him reach for his pocket and pull out a cigarette case in the half-light. A brief flash of silver. He snapped it open and lit a cigarette. As he closed it, she caught two initials. A.K. She inclined her head but said nothing.

"The cell has been compromised," he said, taking another draw of the cigarette.

Claire stiffened and nodded to herself. She placed the accent. Lowland Scot. She reached for the chair across from him but did not sit. "How do you know?"

"Matelot is dead. The SS were waiting for him."

She said nothing in the silence. Matelot... she had that name as one of her contacts, Jacques Morel, a dock worker. She swore under her breath and clenched her fists. The weight of the words settled in the smoky atmosphere.

"Anyone else?"

"Two others. Vigneron and Renard. Their bodies were left as a warning."

Claire exhaled slowly, steadying herself. Henri Dufresne and Simone Berthier.

"Did they give anything away?"

"Fortunately not, they were killed trying to escape, so the SS have nothing more to go on. But..."

"But what?"

"You need to look within."

She nodded. And felt foolish as he wouldn't see in this darkness.

Vanguard slid an envelope across the table, and she reached for it. Its edges curled from the damp. She held it, feeling the paper in her fingers.

"Clos-Léon is compromised now. You cannot go back there. The pilots were captured. The other pilots further down the line must be moved tonight. Those are the papers they will need. They are good."

"I'll take care of it. And you?"

"I will contact you when I need to. Same as today."

Without further ado, he stood, moving like a shadow. His exit was as silent as his arrival.

Claire tucked the envelope into her coat and waited a few minutes to let him get clear before following, descending the stairs to the café below. She nodded to Marguerite and walked to the door, looking up at the rain falling steadily, drenching the street and anyone walking along it. She sighed and pulled her coat close about her body as she stepped out into the night. The streets were empty now, silent under the blackout. She pulled her coat tighter and walked quickly. There was no time to hesitate. There was work to do.

**

Franz Richter's Office, Rouen, Autumn 1941

Franz Richter's office was minimal, with maps of the city pinned to the walls, a heavy wooden desk covered in reports, and a single window overlooking the street. Upon first seeing it, Vogel thought it was much like a police incident room, which was no surprise to him as Franz Richter was a police officer in Hamburg before the war, specialising in murder and organised crime. He was a precise man who followed the evidence and maintained an air of detachment.

When the Nazis came to power, Richter wasn't a true believer. However, being a pragmatist rather than an idealist, like many Germans at the time, he viewed the party as a means of advancement and joined the SS, where he excelled. He transferred to the Sicherheitsdienst, where his investigative experience made him valuable. Unlike some of his more fanatical counterparts, Richter remained professional, preferring surgical precision over brutality, which is why his response to Resistance attacks involved using counterintelligence rather than the Gestapo's favoured method of rounding up groups of civilians and having them shot. Nevertheless, he faced political pressure to do so and sometimes complied if the attack was significant enough. All this did, however, Richter surmised, was strengthen the resistance rather than undermine it. The evidence, he once remarked, spoke for itself.

His role overseeing Rouen required the same methodical approach he had applied during his time in the police force. He used the same principles: eliminate problems efficiently, with minimal disruption, believing that a scalpel is more effective than a sledgehammer. His approach was orderly and disciplined. He kept his office as immaculate and orderly as his mind, his reports concise, and his methods direct.

Vogel had come to know Richter's methods through his work with him since his arrival in Rouen. It occurred to him that Richter would be a dangerous opponent if crossed—not because of blind ideology but because he was rational, adaptable, and difficult to deceive.

Outside the window, Richter watched an army patrol move through the streets, honking horns and shouting orders to move sullen, recalcitrant locals off the street and out of its path. Resistance, he thought, came in many guises, even little ones such as this. They knew what they were doing; he could read their sullen, recalcitrant minds, and part of him admired them. Were their roles reversed, he would do the same. Pouring tiny grains of sand in the gears of the war machine could be as effective as guns and bullets.

He stubbed out his cigarette. He was smoking too much, he thought. He always did when under pressure, and the recent spate of killings was proving a headache and one that needed action. He was, however, at odds with the Gestapo and the Wehrmacht over it.

There was a knock on the door that he was expecting.

"Come."

Untersturmführer Vogel pushed open the door and entered. As always, his uniform was pristine, with his cap worn at a slightly rakish angle that annoyed Richter, but he said nothing. The man was effective, so he was prepared to overlook the little act of vanity bordering on insubordination. Vogel's expression was unreadable. Richter sat, flipping through a dossier, and looked up as Vogel came in, stopped, and snapped a salute. Richter raised a hand, acknowledging the salute.

"Close the door, Untersturmführer, and sit down."

Vogel took off his cap and sat opposite. "You seem troubled, Herr Obersturmführer."

Richter gestured to the file in front of him.

"I am, Untersturmführer."

***

Vogel thought his face was drawn, and his hair looked a little greyer at the temples as he watched Richter sigh and light another cigarette. The smoke curled into the already dense atmosphere of the office. He watched as Richter smoked silently for a moment or two. Eventually, he spoke, and Vogel remained mute, waiting.

"You are aware, Untersturmführer, that the Wehrmacht has been losing soldiers lately?"

Vogel nodded. "I had heard something of it, Herr Obersturmführer. I believe the resistance has been using women to lure their soldiers into cafés, bars, and even brothels. Once on the hook, the fools are taken somewhere quiet and executed. Have I summed up the situation accurately?"

Richter smiled at Vogel's insolent and dismissive tone.

"The Wehrmacht officers are furious, Vogel. They see this as dishonourable. However, the Gestapo sees it as a calculated, effective tactic. I am inclined on this occasion to agree with the Gestapo."

Vogel smiled at the underlying grudging agreement with the thugs of the Gestapo. Like Richter, he had no love for them, so the acquiescence to the point was ironic and amusing to him.

Richter sighed. "We found the body of an Unteroffizier," he looked at the document on this desk, "Ernst Pähtz in an alleyway this morning. Stabbed from behind. We can only speculate what he was up to and why he was so easily taken by surprise. Going by the state of the body, he was much the worse for drink."

"I see."

"Vogel, this is clearly a coordinated effort and is carefully planned. Whatever, we need to do something about it before it escalates out of our control. The Gestapo want to round up civilians." He sighed. "You and I know this will not work, so we need to do something quickly to put a stop to it." He stubbed out his cigarette and opened the silver case, taking another and putting it to his lips. He offered the case to Vogel, who took one and shared the light.

"Initially, Herr Obersturmführer," he said, drawing on the cigarette, "I suggest we tighten security and restrict soldiers from frequenting certain establishments. Then we use informants to find out who these people are."

"We need arrests, Vogel, and quickly. A few executions will concentrate minds and discourage further attacks. What is it the natives here say, *pour encourager les autres*?"

Vogel arched an eyebrow. "Voltaire, Herr Obersturnführer."

Richter shrugged. "Whatever, Vogel. I need action on this sooner rather than later."

Indeed. However, I have a thought about what we can do. A, what you might call, more surgical approach."

"What are you thinking?"

"Put a man on the inside. Infiltrate the cell, then we can make arrests and, well, as you say, some public executions will have a deterrent effect.

"Interesting. Dangerous for the man if he is caught, but that is the risk. You have someone in mind?"

"I do. Once we infiltrate the network, we can identify and remove the key players quietly."

"Then we have our executions."

"Then we have our executions," Vogel said.

Richter stubbed his cigarette firmly, indicating the meeting was ending. "Just bring me results, Herr Untersturmführer."

Vogel stood, clicked his heels and gave a crisp salute. He hesitated slightly, almost imperceptibly. "Heil Hitler," he said.

"Heil Hitler."

He walked out into the hallway and paused briefly, thinking about his next move. He knew the resistance was evolving, becoming more ruthless, but so was he. He had to move quickly now. He smiled. Unbeknownst to Richter, he already had an informant lined up. Time, he decided to put on some pressure.

***

Vogel had Schäfer drive him to the outskirts of Rouen. By the banks of the Seine, he signalled Schäfer to stop next to an abandoned warehouse. He put a raincoat over his uniform and left his cap in the car as he stepped out, putting up an umbrella to keep off the interminable rain.

"Wait here."

"Yes, Herr Untersturmführer."

Schäfer settled back and took out a packet of cigarettes from his top pocket and lit a smoke. It occurred to him that driving Vogel about was an easy job and saved fighting on the front line. He intended to make the most of it.

Vogel splashed his way across the broken ground to the entrance of the building and walked inside.

The place was dimly lit with shafts of light from the small windows near the rafters. Puddles of water lay on the old concrete floor, and he could hear drips coming through the gaps in the roof as they landed in the puddles. Even now, in its deserted state, there was a faint smell of oil from machinery that was long gone. He paused for a moment as he heard engines. Aircraft flying overhead. He frowned and waited. They passed by, and he relaxed again.

Further inside, a single oil lamp flickered on a crate where a man sat waiting. He looked up when he heard the door being pulled aside and watched Vogel walk towards him with measured steps, scanning the shadows as he did so. He trusted no one, especially not someone under his control. His uniform was a target, and he was aware of his vulnerability, being so far from the city's centre and alone. If the man he was meeting were so inclined, an ambush would be simple. However, he saw no signs of a threat, so he carried on walking.

His informant sat, mute, on the crate, watching, waiting like a prey animal awaiting its fate. The low light partially obscured his face. He stood as Vogel drew closer and nodded.

"Herr Untersturmführer…"

Vogel slowly removed his gloves, watching the man and dispensed with niceties. "We have a problem," he said.

"We do?"

"I have just come from Herr Obersturmführer Richter. He is becoming concerned about the executions of Wehrmacht soldiers in Rouen. Something needs to be done. If not, the Gestapo will start rounding up civilians. I think neither of us would like to see such a distasteful outcome, don't you agree?"

"Of course not."

"Richter wants swift, precise action. This resistance cell is to be dismantled and eliminated. We will have executions, but not innocent civilians. You understand?"

The man said nothing. His body tensed, and he waited for Vogel to finish.

"That means you, my friend. I need names. Locations. And soon. So you must infiltrate. Become a part of the cell."

The informant nodded but hesitated. "They are careful. They trust no one. It will be dangerous, Herr Untersturmführer."

"Of course, it will be dangerous. This is a dangerous world, and remember, we can eliminate your wife and child if we so wish."

"Where are they?"

"They are safe enough. For the moment. How long that remains the case is up to you, my friend."

The man tensed at the familiarity, and his mouth twisted, but he refrained from voicing his thoughts.

"Trust is earned," Vogel said, continuing as if the response had never happened. "You do what is necessary to become indispensable to them."

"I will need something."

"Of course. There is an abandoned tailor shop, Mercerie Dupont, on the Rue Saint-Sever. You know of it?"

"Yes, wasn't it owned by Jews? They disappeared…"

"Yes, that is the one. The Gestapo never registered the building. Anyway, it would make a useful safe house. Except, of course, you and I know that it is not safe. I will have listening devices in place."

"Of course."

"If they suspect you, you know what will happen."

"I am between the devil and the sea."

Vogel shrugged. "Maybe you shouldn't have married a Jew, eh?"

"And when this is done? What then? Will I be free? Will you release Yvette?"

Vogel took out his cigarette case and offered one to the informant, who shook his head. Vogel shrugged, placed one in his lips, and lit it. He drew deeply on it, narrowing his eyes as he looked at the man entangled in his web. For a fleeting moment, he felt something. What was it? Guilt? Empathy? Sorrow? He wasn't sure as it came and went in a flash, so quickly that it almost never happened. He shrugged the thought away. "You'll have what was promised," he said. He dropped his voice to a whisper. "But fail me, and I will ensure you disappear before the resistance can deal with you, and so will your Jewess."

The informant sighed, nodding. "I'll get what you need. How do I know you will keep your promise?"

"You don't," Vogel said. He dropped his cigarette on the floor and ground it out. He looked about out of habit, but they were still alone. "Wait until I am gone." With that, he turned and walked back to the door.

Outside, it was still raining. The sky was darker as the invisible sun set somewhere in the west. He shrugged and climbed into the car, heading back to the city. He trusted that his informant would do as asked. The man had no choice. But if it all went wrong, he was expendable.

Chapter 8

Lodève, Present Day

Clarice looked up from her computer as François Viala entered through the main door.

"Clarice," he said. "*Bonjour*. Are the others here?"

Clarice shook her head. "Monsieur Radfield is in Edinburgh. Monsieur Laurent and Madame are on their way. They will be here shortly. Can I get you anything or help you in any way while we are waiting?"

"A coffee would be appreciated."

Clarice busied herself getting a coffee ready. While she was doing that, Viala looked around the office. "Have you gone any further with the investigation?"

"Some progress, *Capitaine*, yes. We have discovered that a British agent was working with Claire Lemoine. We have also found some evidence relating to Monsieur Defrense's uncle. He was in the same resistance cell. Not much further than that. However, someone is watching us. Monsieur Radfield telephoned yesterday evening to say that he was followed on his way back to his hotel."

"Ah, yes, that is what I want to talk about. I will wait for the others to get here."

She had just finished when Patrice and Pascale came through the door. "François," Pascale said, reaching out to kiss him on each cheek. "Come on through." He took the coffee Clarice handed him and followed them to the back office.

He dropped into a chair, placed his cup on the table, and rubbed his face, clearly exhausted. "It's over," he said. "My investigation has been shut down."

Pascale and Patrice exchange a look. Pascale frowned. "Who?"

Viala shook his head. "Internal Security. Orders came from high up. You know what those people are like. You've had investigations shut down in your time when you found yourself too close to the intelligence people." He shrugged. "We can do nothing."

"Well, it was natural causes," Patrice said. "I know there are suspicious circumstances, but I can see their point of view."

"I am convinced there was something else going on, but I was treading on toes, and someone is getting twitchy, given what has happened to Monsieur Radfield. How is he, by the way?"

Patrice looked at Pascale, and she nodded.

"He is in Edinburgh…"

"On his way to Berlin now," Clarice interrupted.

"Sorry, yes, Berlin. Anyway, last night, he told us he was being followed. That is no coincidence." He glanced at the documents on the table. "Whatever we are stumbling into, it's dangerous. And now they want it buried."

"Did they give you a reason?" Pascale said

Viala gave a dry laugh that was more of a bark and sipped his coffee. "No. Just a warning to 'redirect my resources elsewhere.' I spoke to the commandant, and he gave me strict orders to drop it or else, so I'm dropping it."

"Are you?" she said.

Viala hesitated, then leaned forward. "I'm off the case officially. But unofficially, I take a dim view of spooks giving me orders, and that was my suspicious death." He lowered his voice. "Watch yourselves. Someone's already cleaning this up, and they don't care who gets in the way."

Silence. The weight of his words settled in the room.

Viala finished his coffee. "I'll help you if I can, but officially? You never spoke to me."

Patrice nodded. "Understood, François."

"And you?"

"We carry on. The spooks can stop you officially. We can afford to be more resistant."

"Well, be careful." Viala stood. "Time I wasn't here. He buttoned his coat and hesitated at the door. "As I say, take care of yourselves. They have tried once to kill Radfield. Keep a watch out."

He left, closing the door behind him, leaving Pascale and Patrice staring at each other, knowing things had just escalated.

"Coffee?" Clarice said.

***

The Bundesarchiv, Berlin, Present Day

Berlin was wet. The rain fell in a steady drizzle as Radfield made his way from the hotel to the Bundesarchiv. He kept an eye on his surroundings but saw no sign of a tail as he walked along the wet pavement, dodging the umbrellas of office workers, heads down, drearily walking to their daily drudge. He was grateful when he reached the building and stepped inside, shaking some of the rain from his coat. He stopped to wipe the dampness from his glasses, which promptly steamed up. Looking about, he saw the reception desk, walked across, and introduced himself.

He waited until someone came to collect him.

"Herr Radfield?" A blonde woman in her early thirties held out her hand. "I am Ingrid Keller."

"Pleased to meet you," he said, taking the proffered hand. "We spoke yesterday?"

"Yes, that was me. Please follow me. I have sorted out some files for you to look at." She led him to a quiet room with rows of desks where scholars hunched over old documents. The air smelled of dust, aged paper, and ink. A faint hum from overhead lights added to the sterile stillness.

Once Radfield was seated, Ingrid gave him a stack of carefully catalogued files and warned him to handle them carefully. "Please wear these gloves while handling them," she said, holding out a pair of white cotton gloves. Radfield took them and put them on. "Some records were lost during the war, but you may find what you're looking for. One thing the Nazis were renowned for was their meticulous record keeping."

"Useful for historians," Radfield said. "Although at present, I am more interested in the Weimar Republic. The Nazi era may come later, depending on what I uncover."

"That was a little more chaotic," she said, "but see what you can find. I'm here if you need me."

She left him alone. He glanced up at a large clock on the wall, which ticked steadily as he opened the first file.

Here we go.

He leafed through the files in silence. Outside, he could hear the distant hum of the city, but inside, there was only the tapping of keyboards, the sound of pages being turned and the occasional murmur of researchers.

He started looking for James Kerr's academic history—school records, university enrolment, and anything that placed him in Germany from around 1920 onwards. At first, he found nothing unusual. Immigration records showed that he entered the country with his mother in late 1921. He carried on working through the pages of files. He flipped a page and froze.

Ah. This is interesting.

He had found a school record for James Kerr in Frankfurt.

"Well," he muttered to himself. "You weren't just visiting." As he worked through the records, he found grades, attendance, and subject focus. Radfield's German was weak, unlike his grasp of French, so he took his time, making notes and taking photographs as he went.

"Hmm. Fluent in German. I'd expect that. Exceptional in history and languages. Much like our Claire—German, French, English. Very useful for an agent in the field. Oh, what's this?"

According to the record, Kerr's attendance was sponsored by a benefactor. "*Kulturverein für Heimkehr.*" Radfield tapped his pen against the table. "This isn't just an ordinary education record. Someone wanted you to be here, James." He scribbled the name down in his notepad.

He walked back to Ingrid Keller. "What do you have on," he looked at his notes, "the *Kulturverein für Heimkehr, frauline*?"

Ingrid frowned and took the note. "During the Weimar Republic, several organisations were formed to encourage and help the German diaspora overseas to relocate back to Germany. This looks like one of them. I am not sure, Herr Radfield, but I can look into it for you, if you wish."

"Yes, please, it would help put a few pieces of the jigsaw together."

He went back to his desk and checked further into the records. There was nothing after the school and no mention of a university. Did he return to Britain? Stay in Germany? Then, another name caught his attention. Heinrich Vogel. "That name rings a bell." He thought about it, but try as he might, the reference didn't come back. He made a note. "It'll come back to me later, no doubt."

Radfield took out his phone and was about to take photographs of the relevant files. There was a photograph of Kerr taken in 1929. A tall, gangly young man with cropped sandy hair and a lopsided smile. Radfield focused the phone camera and copied the image. It wasn't great, he told himself, but it would suffice. They knew what Vanguard looked like as an adolescent. He smiled and looked up.

Bugger. Not again.

Someone was watching him. At the far end of the room, a man was pretending to read but glancing his way too often. He sighed and closed the file, slipping his notepad and phone into his pocket. He stood and looked about. He couldn't see any other people watching, just the one.

"Time I wasn't here."

His phone rang.

"Patrice?"

"How are things going, David?"

"I'm being watched again."

"*D'accord*. Be careful. When were you planning on leaving the records office?"

"About now. Why?"

"Well, it may be something, or it may not. I've been going through Claire's diary. Have you found anything relating to Franz Richter? He was the SS officer in charge at Rouen until 1943. He was involved in a couple of nasty reprisals in 1941 and 1942."

"What happened in 1943?"

"He was assassinated. The records here seem somewhat vague. I wondered if you might find anything more concrete relating to why the resistance wanted to kill him."

"Okay, I'm on it. It might be worth checking the SOE records as well. Could Clarice contact the UK records for anything more they might have?"

"On it."

"Oh, one other thing," Radfield said. "It might be nothing..."

"Go on..."

"Well, Kerr had a sponsor, the *Kulturverein für Heimkehr*, while he was at school. There aren't any details that I could see in those files. I wonder if there is anything in the SOE files. It does look as if he was recruited as a teenager."

"Scottish, German speaker, yes, I could see that would be of interest to the intelligence services. Look, David, you get back here as soon as you can. I'll ask Clarice to contact the archives in London and see if they have anything on this benefactor."

He put everything away and went back to the desk. "*Fraüline,*" he said. "I am running out of time. I wonder if it's possible that someone here can look up some information for us?"

Keller smiled. "Of course, Herr Radfield. That is my job. I would be delighted to help. This investigation of yours sounds exciting. What exactly do you need?"

"Anything you can find on the *Kulturverein für Heimkehr* and anything relating to the assassination of Obersturmfürher Franz Richter in 1943."

"Of course," Keller said, making notes as he spoke.

"Here is my colleague's card. If you find anything of use, please contact her." He gave her Clarice's business card.

"Certainly, Herr Radfield. A little research breaks up the day."

The Camargue, Present Day

It was Sunday, and Pascale took her usual ride out to the Camargue. She parked the FTR and took her packed lunch from the messenger bag strapped to the side frame. She walked along the salt marshes briefly before finding a place to sit down. Since marrying Patrice, she retained this habit of riding off alone to the Camargue. It was a retreat where she could meditate and spend time with her thoughts; sometimes those thoughts were with Guillaume. The death of a partner is always unfinished business, she felt. Whereas Patrice was divorced and had a degree of closure, the death of a partner left a hole that her new husband would never fully understand, despite his attempts to do so. Consequently, she took time out to ride and be alone with her thoughts and her past. She sighed as she watched the flamingos coming and going.

She was hungry. Lunch was somewhat delayed, and now it was late afternoon. The light painted the water in hues of gold and pink. The only sound was the cries of the Flamingos as they waded through the shallows, their long necks curving as they picked through the brine. The wind carried the scent of salt and wild lavender. She breathed deeply. When she needed time to think, this was her retreat. No one else came here. No distractions. No phone calls and, she noted, no one had followed her from Lodève.

She sat and chewed the baguette, allowing her mind to wander. So far, the investigation had thrown up leads that seemed to go nowhere. More disturbing was François's news. Bigger players were involved, and the attempt on Radfield and Laurence worried her. The pieces of the puzzle didn't fit, and she felt they were missing something vital. She watched the flamingos, seeking clarity in their quiet, rhythmic movements. Why would the intelligence services be bothered about Defrense's death?

"Here again?"

She looked up; Geneviève was beside her, standing at the water's edge, hands in her pockets, looking out across the water. She never changed. While Pascale wore the years since Geneviève died in the lines around her eyes and the silver streaks in her dark hair, Geneviève remained frozen in time. A young woman cut off in her thirties. She wore the lilac coat, bobble hat, purple skirt, and boots she wore that last fatal day. As always, she was calm and composed, her presence at once comforting and unsettling.

"You are here again, too," Pascale said. "I thought you had gone now."

"You always come here when you need to think. And I do love the flamingos," Geneviève said. "So what is the problem now?"

"Something doesn't add up. We find snippets of information that don't make sense. That lead nowhere. We have a mysterious agent, Vanguard, who now has a name, but precious little else on the man. We have evidence of my grandmother in France. But she wasn't among the bodies recovered in the Pyrenees, so we are no closer to finding out what happened to her. Or Vanguard, for that matter. And François Viala's investigation has been shut down. Although," she paused, "I can understand that one. Lucien's death was from natural causes, so there's no murder suspect, just some vague clues hinting at someone being there at the time. The likelihood of a criminal conviction is next to zero. Viala is annoyed, though. Out of principle. He doesn't take kindly to the intelligence services interfering."

"You already know who shut down François's investigation. Just not why."

"Yes. Why? Most of the people involved will be dead by now, anyway. Who are they trying to protect? Or," She paused again, "Or, we are looking at this from the wrong angle." She looked at Geneviève, who was grinning. "I'm right, aren't I? This isn't about 'who', it's about '*why*.'" She looked back out at the flamingos who were still absorbed in their hunt for food.

"Maybe the answer is simpler than you think."

Pascale turned sharply. "Do you know?"

"It doesn't work that way, you know that. Perhaps you just need to listen to yourself more. Think. Follow the trail. Look at the clues you already have. See what Radfield turns up in Berlin."

"That worries me too. He has been followed over there as well."

"Radfield can look after himself."

Pascale exhaled, turning to speak again, only to find Geneviève gone. Just the flamingos remained, unbothered by the shifting world around them.

"*Merde*! Why do you always do that?"

The thought Geneviève planted lingered. Pascale closed her eyes and focused. The answer is there. She just had to find it. She harrumphed and finished her sandwich. Whatever it was, it wasn't coming now. It would, when she least expected it.

Just as she was preparing to start the bike, her phone rang. Sighing, she unbuckled her helmet and fished it out of her pocket.

"*Âllo?*"

"Madame Hervé, it's Étienne Caron..."

"Yes, of course. To what do I owe the pleasure, doctor?"

"There's been an interesting development. We have found another body."

***

Lodève, Present Day

Clarice was alone in the office, as seemed to be the case lately. With Radfield in Germany, Patrice in Paris and Pascale on her way to Pau, she was left to keep the office open, field enquiries from potential clients and dig around online for anything that might be of use to the others. She was busy with this when the office phone rang. She picked it up.

"François, how are you?"

"Busy on another investigation, Clarice. However, as promised, I did some digging around using my resources. If I ever get caught, this conversation never took place."

"Understood."

"The names you had for the resistance cell. I may have found something for you."

"Go on."

"The Fourniers had a son. Jacques. He was about ten or eleven at the time. He disappeared off the radar after the war. I have been looking through police files, but I've drawn a blank. You might find something if you go to the *Archives Nationales*. I would, but I don't have the time."

Clarice put the phone down and called Patrice.

"Where are you at the moment, Patrice?"

"I've just finished digging through Resistance files before I return to Lodève, why?"

"François called. Apparently, the Fourniers had a son. Jacques. François got no further, but if you are there, you might find something. Oh, hang on..."

"What?"

"While we were talking, I was doing a search on records I found online the other day. I think I have what we need. Check for Artur Giraud. I found a file here that says he was effectively a ward of the state."

"I'll look into it and send you what I find."

***

Clarice put the phone on the desk and returned to her computer screen. She was chasing a story. "Ah," she said to herself, "this looks interesting." She read through it and stopped for a moment, staring at the document. "My god." She picked up the phone again.

"Clarice, what is it?"

"Monsieur, you might want to look at this, I'm sending you a link."

"What is it?"

"I don't know if it is related to our case, but the Nazis carried out a mass execution in Rouen in 1941. Our Untersturmführer Vogel's name crops up."

She waited while Patrice had a chance to look at the link she sent. "Hmm, maybe. Keep a note of it. I don't know if it's relevant or not at this stage. Print out the report, and put it on the corkboard with the rest. If there's a link, fair enough."

***

Café Lys Noir, Rouen, 1941

André Fournier was wiping down tables when he heard the commotion. Shouts, running feet, the sudden roar of engines. He looked up just as a *Kübelwagen* tore past the café, followed by the screech of brakes and the crack of gunfire. Then, loud banging on doors, and shouted commands in German.

"Marguerite, get down here, there's something happening outside."

Marguerite came running through from the back, her apron still tied around her waist, and joined him by the door, where they pulled back the net curtain and peered out. The SS and Wehrmacht were banging on doors and breaking them down when they didn't get an answer. Men, women and even a teenager were being dragged out into the streets and lined up under guard, with rifles at their necks.

André's stomach turned. "Richter and Vogel," he said. "What the Hell is this?"

In the small square outside, the soldiers were erecting makeshift gallows with practised efficiency: a small platform, two uprights, a crossbeam, and ropes. Once they were complete, the prisoners were marched to the base of them.

"*Merde!*" Marguerite said, her hand going to her mouth. "That's the whole of Les Silhouettes. I can't watch." She turned her head away.

Despite his horror, André watched as the dozen prisoners were dragged onto the gallows, standing on a small platform. Once they were all lined up, a sergeant barked an order, and the platform was kicked away. The bodies dropped.

Their legs jerked and thrashed.

Then they went still.

Richter picked up a megaphone. "The next time resistance groups murder a German soldier, we will not only hang those involved, we will hang their families. This stops now."

Then, in a roar of engines and diesel fumes, the German vehicles drove off, leaving the gallows with its victims dangling silently in the winter sunshine.

"That's the whole cell," Marguerite said. "My God. All of them, gone."

André watched, his fists clenching and unclenching in silent rage. "The Bosche will pay, Marguerite, don't worry about that. We will make them pay."

"But all of them. How?"

André shook his head. "I don't know. But…"

"But what?"

He looked at her and saw the tears in her eyes, that matched the lump in his own throat. Those people were friends they had known all their lives. Colleagues and allies. "I can only suspect that they were betrayed," he said. "We all need to be doubly careful now."

***

Franz Richter's Office, Rouen, 1941

Vogel knocked on the door.

"Come."

He pushed the door open, walked over to Richter's desk, clicked his heels, and snapped a salute: "Heil Hitler."

Richter raised an arm lethargically. "Heil Hitler. Please, sit." He then returned to the papers on his desk while Vogel sat.

Vogel went through the ritual of opening his silver cigarette case, putting a cigarette in his mouth, cupping the end, and lighting it. He patiently waited for Richter's attention as the man busied himself signing documents before looking up.

"Well, Herr Untersturmführer, while that little episode the other day was regrettable. I dislike reprisals, as you know, but at least we had the perpetrators, so it was justified. I wanted to take the opportunity to congratulate you on a job well done. Your intelligence was sound, and I am very pleased with the results."

Vogel sat back and blew a stream of smoke into the air, looking toward the window as he heard the sound of engines go by, then back at Richter. "A satisfactory outcome, Her Obersturmführer. We have rooted out one cell, that is all."

"And your informant?"

"So far, no one appears to suspect him, although they will be suspicious of everyone by now."

Richter nodded. "Well, be that as it may, Vogel, for the moment, I think we can give the Wehrmacht some assurance that their soldiers will not be executed on their leave time, eh?"

Vogel smiled and stubbed his cigarette out in the ashtray. "Time will tell, Herr Obersturmführer. If not random killings of Wehrmacht soldiers out getting drunk, then they will find something else. This will be a lull, nothing more, I suspect."

Richter nodded. "I am not naïve enough to think any different, Herr Untersturmführer. But we make the most of the lull while it lasts."

"Indeed, Herr Obersturmführer."

"Dismissed."

Vogel stood, repeated the crisp salute and walked out, adjusting his cap to just the right rakish angle that irritated Richter.

***

Malaunay, January 1942

The hour before dawn. A mist hung across the viaduct. André made his way slowly down the slope, the backpack full of charges making it an unsteady progress to the track where the tunnel ended and the viaduct began. He looked up where Jean-Luc was watching. He raised his head in question, and Jean-Luc nodded.

Okay to go, then.

He secured a line, swung over the parapet, and abseiled down just below the arches. Dangling from the rope, he packed the Nobel 808 charges against the central struts of the viaduct, working efficiently as everything had to be in place before the sun came up. He wedged the charges into place with steel clips and packed the seams with mud. The pencil fuses gave them ten minutes. Again, he looked up. Across the eastern sky he could see the first faint streaks of grey. Jean-Luc gave a thumbs-up. Ten minutes, just enough time to return to the treeline and vanish into the trees before sunrise. Despite the early morning cold, he felt sweat trickling down his neck.

He tried to forget his fear and focused on the work and his burning anger, pent up since the executions a few weeks previously. Then, having finished, he looked around and, satisfied, he climbed back up the rope onto the track. He looked up at Jean-Luc, who gestured for him to run.

"Come on, André! It will be here any minute."

As if on cue, he could hear the faint creaking in the rails as the train approached.

Needing no extra encouragement, he pounded up the slope where the others were waiting. Claire and Marguerite held their Sten guns close. Marguerite handed André another gun.

"Jean-Luc, you go back along the way and wait. Keep an eye out for any Bosche that might come along the road."

He nodded and left into the semi-darkness.

Then they heard the whistle from the other side of the tunnel and a rumble of the approaching train. Claire looked at her comrades. She felt the tension, but none of them showed it.

"Once the train goes, we mop up as agreed."

The other two nodded.

"Then we make for the safe house. Split up and go separately, yes?"

Again, nods. They had been through this several times. Everyone knew their roles. This was just that final boost, she told herself—something to take away the taste in her mouth.

The train whistled again as it entered the tunnel. She looked at her watch.

Any moment now.

Then, just as the grey fingers of dawn cast their eerie light across the valley and the sun poked its bleary face over the horizon, in a swirl of smoke and steam, the train thundered out of the tunnel and onto the viaduct just as the first charge blew. There was a flash, bang, and crack as the stones gave way, and then another and another, and the viaduct started to buckle. The tracks gave way with it, and the train was hurled out into the air above the valley. It seemed to hang there like a gigantic flying monster before gravity took over, and it plunged to the ground, the boiler exploding on impact, throwing shards of hot metal into the air. The carriages followed, one after another, throwing men and postbags to their deaths below.

"Now! Go! For *La Silhouettes*!" Claire said. They ran down to the wreckage. Most of the soldiers were inert, but some stood and reached for their weapons. The air was filled with the sound of the chattering Sten guns as they mowed down the survivors. The odour of burning metal, cordite and steam filled Claire's nostrils as she braced against the recoil of the weapon spraying death across the field, her face a grimace of vengeance and anger.

Then it was over. Silence apart from the hissing of the dying locomotive breathing its last.

"Let's get out of here," she said.

The others needed no second prompt. One after another, they vanished like wraiths into the trees.

Claire ran, her breath coming in gasps, the Sten gun heavy on its strap that rubbed her shoulder, and the metal bumped against her hip. She constantly pulled on the strap to alleviate the discomfort, and all the time, a thought ran through her mind.

Something is wrong here.

She didn't know what, and couldn't pin it down, but something about the morning's work didn't fit. She kept running, making her way to the outskirts of the town, where the safe house was. Reaching it, she stopped and looked about, breathing heavily. It was light now and she expected some signs of life as people went to the boulangerie to buy bread, but nothing. No sign of anyone. She snatched open the door and went inside. Up the stairs and into the attic, pulling the trap door shut behind her.

The Fourniers were already there.

"Jean-Luc?" André said.

She shook her head. "I've not seen him since the explosion. I waited by the trees briefly, but didn't see him."

"What were we supposed to be blowing up this morning?" Marguerite said.

Claire shook her head. "We were supposed to be blowing a troop and ammo train, but that wasn't. I don't know."

"Where did you get the intelligence?" André said, his voice rising slightly.

"Vanguard."

They stood in silence as they thought about the implications.

"Maybe he got it wrong," Claire said. "A change of schedule."

"That train was just post and documents with a few guards. We may have caused inconvenience with the viaduct, but there were no troops or ammunition. It was too easy. There were only a few Bosche."

"I know."

"We need to ask Vanguard," Margarite said.

Claire nodded. "Yes. In the meantime, we stay here and hope the Gestapo don't find us."

They tensed when they heard footsteps coming up the stairs. The hatch slid back, and the old man who owned the house put his head up into the opening. "Well, you made a good mess this morning. The Bosche are looking everywhere for you." He paused, eyes narrowing. "Where is the other one?"

Claire shook her head. "We got separated. We don't know."

"Well, let's hope he isn't captured, or we will all be done for. Why did you blow up a post train? I thought it was supposed to be soldiers you were killing?"

"I know. Something went wrong with our information."

"Huh! Well, I hope it was worth it, because they won't take it lying down, just you wait and see. What are you going to do now?"

"Wait here until tomorrow night, then move out."

"*D'accord*. Keep quiet if the Bosche come calling, eh?"

***

Later that evening, the old man returned bearing some stale bread and cheese. "Best I could do in the circumstances," he said, his voice curt.

Claire took it, and they sat in silence while they ate the meagre meal. The room was heavy with unspoken recrimination.

"Still no sign of Jean-Luc," Marguerite said at one point. No one answered. By now, they assumed the worst. But no knock on the door. Nothing.

The following morning, dawn pushed its grey light through the window, and Claire walked over to look out. Below, she could see the small town square. As she watched, several trucks roared into it and came to a halt. SS-Sicherheitsdienst poured out, running from door to door, dragging people out into the square. She could hear shouts and some small arms fire.

André came up and stood next to her. "Those two. I know them. Richter and Vogel. They were there when *La Silhouettes* were executed."

Richter was shouting orders, while Vogel stood watching, saying nothing. Ten people were lined up and machine-gunned. Claire gasped and stepped back from the window, her hand over her mouth to stifle the sound.

"Yes," André said. That's what it was like watching *La Silhouettes* being executed. He continued to watch. "They are bringing the mayor out," he said. "Oh, my God."

"What?"

"They just hanged the poor blighter from a lamp post."

Claire slumped to the floor. "We did this."

"I know," Marguerite said. "We always knew this would happen. We are at war. This is what happens in war."

"I know. I know. But, it doesn't make it any easier."

Marguerite shook her head. "No. It never gets easier."

Later that day, the hatch slid open, and they started at the noise. Jean-Luc clambered into the small space. "I was delayed."

"We noticed," Claire said. "What happened?"

"Bosche everywhere, I had to lie low and wait until the patrols had passed. I saw the square." He swore. "There are several buildings on fire, too. The Bosche are taking this one badly."

"Did you see Richter or Vogel?" André said.

Jean-Luc shook his head. "No, there were no Bosche about when I came though. They have all gone."

They waited until nightfall and slipped out into the dark, making their way back to Rouen.

"I need to speak to Vanguard about this," Claire said.

"I know. I'll get a message to him," Marguerite said.

***

Café Lys Noir

Claire walked in, closing the door on the cold weather outside, welcoming the warmth after the frosty air. She glanced at Marguerite, who gave her a nod.

"*Bonjour, Chérie.*"

By the time she reached the bar, there was a coffee and a brandy waiting. She leaned against the bar and sipped the brandy, relishing the fiery warmth as it coursed through her, bracing her for what was to come. She looked at Marguerite and raised her eyes upwards towards the ceiling. She was treated to the barest nod before Marguerite turned to deal with a customer. She looked across. The Gestapo officer. The man was a regular, she thought. He looked at her and took off his fedora.

"Madame, I see you are here again."

"Indeed, Herr..."

He smiled, a smile that played on his lips but never quite reached his grey eyes.

"Falkenrath, Klaus Falkenrath." He lifted his brandy to his lips, never taking his eye off her. She felt something crawl up her spine and back down again.

"What can I do for you, Herr Falkenrath?" she said, keeping her voice calm.

"I thought, perhaps, we could have dinner together."

"I am sorry, Herr Falkenrath...."

"Klaus, please."

"Klaus, but as I say. Another day, perhaps?"

"I notice that you spend a great deal of time upstairs," he said. "I wonder who you are entertaining?"

Claire put the brandy glass down and met the man's gaze. Without flinching, despite the turmoil in her stomach, she said, "*Ich bin eine loyale Reichsbürgerin. Ich habe hier Geschäfte, die Sie nichts angehen.*"

He nodded. "I see, Frau, I apologise. Please, if I can be of any assistance."

She nodded. "I know where to find you, Herr Falkenrath. Thankyou for your concern."

He nodded. "Think nothing of it. Maybe another day, I can have the pleasure?"

"Maybe."

He gave the mirthless smile again and returned to his table, where he sat and watched as she walked past the bar to the back of the building, her chest tight with tension.

She went upstairs. Vanguard was already there, his face in shadow, as always. She sat in the chair opposite. For a moment, they sat in silence. Eventually, she spoke.

"That wasn't a troop or arms train."

"No."

"What happened?"

"The intel was flawed."

"That's it? The intel was flawed? What about the people murdered by the SS? What did they die for?"

She heard him sigh. *Exasperation?* she wondered.

"They were going to die anyway. That was always the sacrifice. It's what we do when we fight the enemy."

"For a worthwhile effort, maybe, but for a post train? How can you be so calm?"

He lit a cigarette and drew on it, the silver case catching what little light there was.

"We are fighting a war. Casualties are part of the cost. So, too, is the occasional wrong target. Your training at SOE should have prepared you for this, Claire."

"Nothing prepares you for watching your countrymen lined up and shot in cold blood. They hanged the mayor from a lamp post, for God's sake! Prepared? No, I was not prepared, and thank God I still have enough humanity to be shocked and horrified by what I saw, and it was all for nothing."

He smoked his cigarette in silence for a moment, waiting for her to gather her emotions. "No. Maybe not. But the damage will delay trains for a while, including troop trains. You struck a blow. Not the blow we hoped for, but a blow nonetheless." He stubbed out the cigarette and stood. "I must go now. I'll be in touch." As he reached the door, he paused and turned. "You think that the resistance movement wins wars? No, you don't. All you do is bleed the enemy. It is all you can do. It is all we expect you to do. But that is useful enough. However, someone along the line has to make a call. A call that costs lives, that we know will cost innocent lives. I made that call. I am the one who will live with it. My conscience is clear. There are bigger things in play here. We need to win this war. If a few locals die, then so be it. It's the price we pay. *I pay.*"

He hesitated for a second. His shoulders slumped almost imperceptibly, then he straightened again, pushing the door open.

She watched him go, closing the door behind him.

"You sanctimonious bastard."

***

Rouen, three weeks earlier

Schäfer brought the staff car to a halt and turned in his seat. "You stay here, Sergeant," Vogel said.

"Herr, Untersturmführer."

Schäfer nodded, pulling a cigarette from its packet and lighting it. He leaned back, exhaling as the flame flared.

Vogel pushed open the door and stepped out. He paused, adjusting his coat and tilting his cap to just the right rakish angle. A small smile played across his lips as he glanced back at the driver.

"Don't get too comfortable. I won't be long."

"Very good, Herr Untersturmführer."

Vogel crossed to the warehouse, his breath clouding in the cold air. The metal door screeched as he pushed it open, wincing at the noise. He pulled it closed behind him, sealing out the morning light. Puddles dotted the cracked floor where the roof leaked. He stepped around them carefully, unwilling to soil his polished boots.

His informant sat waiting in a battered chair left behind when whatever business occupied the place vacated it.

"Well," Vogel said without preamble, "what have you got for me?"

The man tensed. Vogel smiled to himself.

"They're planning to take out a troop train. Malaunay."

"When?"

"The twenty-eighth. At dawn."

Vogel nodded. "Do they have a safe house to use after the raid?"

"Yes."

"Give me the details."

"You're going to arrest them?" the man asked.

Vogel took out his silver cigarette case and lit a cigarette, deliberately drawing out the moment. The tension was delicious. Was the man afraid of him, or for his comrades? It didn't matter. Vogel relished the power all the same.

"Maybe. Maybe not." He drew on the cigarette and exhaled a long plume of smoke into the cold air.

"I thought you were going to arrest them. That I'd be off the hook."

Vogel shook his head. "The long game, my dear fellow. The long game. I might have use for your little cell yet. Alive and believing they are in the clear allows me to gather more information, so not yet. Let them run a little longer, thinking they are safe."

The man's face twisted as the realisation dawned: he would never be free of Vogel.

"A troop train, you say?" Vogel mused, almost to himself.

"Yes."

"Hmm. Can't let that happen. I'll need to make some calls."

He dropped the cigarette and crushed it under his heel.

"Very good. I'll be in touch. Don't go anywhere, *alles klar*?"

He turned and walked out, the door clanging shut behind him. The informer watched him go and swore softly under his breath.

***

Richter's Office, 29th January, 1942

"How did this happen?" Richter snapped. "How? I put you in charge of finding these Resistance cells and rooting them out. And so far, all I have to show for it is a disaster that will force me to respond with reprisals. What happened to your informant?"

Vogel shrugged. "He gave us a cell a few weeks ago. We put a stop to the random killings. That slowed things, but I did caution you that pressure would provoke escalation."

"Don't be insubordinate, Herr Untersturmführer."

"Unfortunately, Herr Obersturmführer, he did not come through for me on this occasion. It must have been a different cell. They're like cockroaches—all over the city."

"And it is your job, Herr Untersturmführer, to administer the insecticide. So far, it is you who has been found wanting."

"Herr Obersturmführer."

"Oh, get out!"

Vogel clicked his heels, saluted, and turned to leave.

Richter stared at the map on the wall. "Wait."

Vogel paused. A smile flickered across his lips, quickly wiped away as he turned back with a raised eyebrow.

"Herr Obersturmführer?"

"Make arrangements for us to go to Malaunay," he said, standing and picking up his cap.

Vogel nodded. "*Alles klar*, Herr Obersturmführer."

"*Sheiße*"

***

Pau, Present Day.

By the time Pascale parked her bike, the police had taped off the scene. She walked up to the *guardien* waiting at the entrance to the cordon.

"*Bonjour*, I believe that Doctor Caron is expecting me. Pascale Hervé."

"Yes, madame, he did tell me to expect you." The man lifted the tape and gestured to Pascale to step through. "He is further up the trail, beyond the cave, madame."

Pascale nodded her thanks and walked along the trail that she had walked with Caron a few days previously. The cave entrance was still as it was. She carried on past where the path narrowed and a sheer drop to the left descended by around three hundred meters to a ravine. The slope was littered with boulders and scrubby bushes. Partway down, she saw a group of forensic investigators. Next to them, she saw Caron. He looked up and waved, gesturing for her to come down and join them. holding out a hand to balance herself, Pascale moved carefully down the screelined slope and joined the group.

"Pascale," Caron said, holding out his hand. She shook it.

"Bonjour, Doctor."

Doctor Renauld stood up and held out a hand. "Bonjour, madame. We have another mysterious skeleton."

"What can you tell me?"

Renauld sighed. "As with the others, this is several decades old. The police," he gestured to the officers milling about, "have no interest here now that they know it is not a recent murder."

"But it is a murder?"

"Shot," he said. "Adult male, late twenties or early thirties. He was in good health at the time of death." He crouched down and pointed to the ribcage. "See here, the bone is smashed by a bullet. He was shot in the chest. There are some bones broken that I suspect were post-mortem as he fell."

"Several decades," Pascale said. "The same time period as the others?"

"Yes, I would say so, but..."

She grinned. "Typical pathologist, you are hedging your bets."

"I would hate to get it wrong, madame," he said, winking.

"Do you have any idea of an identity?"

Renauld shook his head. "Not yet. Nothing has shown up in dental records. We can try DNA, but I'm not sure how helpful that would be given that there will be no records."

Caron pointed further down the scree-lined slope. "There are some bits and pieces of debris down there, we think. We will be taking a look later. I'll let you know if we find anything that is of use."

"*D'accord.*"

Pascale looked around her at the stunning scenery, at the cloudless sky, the sheer drops, and the pines reaching above. Somewhere, a bird of prey called out. Once, this was the scene of a murder. Of several murders.

"So, all men. No sign of a woman?"

Caron shook his head. "So far, no."

Pascale sighed. "So I am no further forward with finding *Grand-mère*. I just have another mystery on my hands." She looked down at the remains. "So, who were you?"

Her phone buzzed.

"Clarice, how are things?"

"Madame, I have been doing some digging online and I have found something interesting."

"I like interesting, go on."

"Jacques Fournier."

"Related to our Fourniers?"

She could almost hear the smile down the line. "Indeed, he is. Their son."

"I wonder how the police didn't find him?"

Again, she felt the smile. "Because, madame, he is living under an assumed name. I am sure the *flicks* will get there eventually, but I had a head start. I went back to the *Archives Nationales* and they dug out some useful information. Madame Fournier was executed shortly before the end of the war. Jacques went to live with a couple on the outskirts of Rouen, and it is their property he inherited when they died. There was a note on the file," Pascale heard the pause as Clarice brought up the relevant document on her screen. "Here it is, 'former ward of the state, priority status granted—political reasons.' What do you make of that, madame?"

Pascale sighed heavily. "Someone is hiding something, and they took significant steps to keep it a secret. This is no resistance martyr; there is something deeper going on. That is what I think."

"*D'accord.*"

"Where is he now?"

"Brionne, a few kilometres southwest of Rouen. Do you want to go directly there from Pau?"

"Yes, of course. Text me the address."

***

Lodève, Present Day

Clarice hung up and turned to Patrice. "I may have something of interest for you."

"What is it?"

"Come here, I'll show you." She pointed at her screen. "From what Monsieur Radfield discovered, I did an FOI request in his name. I hope he doesn't mind. Anyway, this is what I got. These are extracts from the military records for the Royal Scots. Look, January 1937, Kerr, James A. 2nd Lieutenant. Royal Scots. So he was back in the United Kingdom then. He is posted for home service.

"Then, moving on, it gets interesting. In January 1938, he is shown as promoted to lieutenant, but with a confidential assignment at the War Office." She looked up at Patrice.

"Military intelligence, by the looks of it. Scroll down."

She did so. "Ah, yes, January 1939, he's missing."

"Keep scrolling. There, 1940. Nothing in the military records. That's when SOE took him over, I suspect. So, where was he from in 1938?"

"I have some other documents. Here is a personnel file. Look what it says, linguistically gifted, politically astute, and highly independent."

"Exactly what the intelligence services would have picked up on. It seems that Vanguard and Claire had a lot in common. What else did you get?"

"A transfer memo. He's showing as being transferred to a special operations unit, section D. What was that?"

"Ah, *D'accord*, that's what we are looking for. Covert operations. That would have been the Secret Intelligence Service that was formed in 1909. It was still called that up until 1940 when SOE was formed. Let's take a closer look."

"Here, with a confidentiality classification." Clarice paused as she scoured the documents. "He monitored German émigrés in the UK and France. Oh. And, here, look, he was transferred to F section, SOE in 1940, just after they were formed, so you were right, Patrice. Oh, and this is where it gets exciting: he is given an alias. Lt. Alexander MacGregor."

Patrice sighed. "Oh, my, now we have a tangled web. Kerr, Krüger and now MacGregor." He picked up his phone. "David."

"Yes?"

"Where are you now?"

"In my hotel. Why?"

"We might have some interesting information that will help you. Did you get anywhere with James Kerr at university?"

"Not so far. I did want to follow that one up."

"Well, we have some information that SOE gave him another alias. I wonder if that might throw anything up your end. Look for anything in Germany that relates to MacGregor."

"I'll look into it, but if SOE gave him that alias, it will be after the time I'm looking at."

He hung up.

Patrice turned back to Clarice's screen. "I have some SOE reports here," she said. "Lt MacGregor parachuted into Germany in autumn 1941. That's interesting that it is Germany. That would have been risky, don't you think? Why didn't he parachute into France if he was working with the resistance?"

"But F section was France, wasn't it?"

"Hmm," Patrice said. "Unless he was embedded in Germany before coming to France."

"Maybe David will find something on that. There must have been a reason for it. Possibly in the redacted stuff we cannot see. That's frustrating."

Clarice looked at the screen. "Here are some reports from him. He notes his meetings with Claire from 1942 onwards. I wonder what he was doing in between."

"Can you send any of this to Pascale?"

"Of course."

"Where is she at the moment?

"Pau. They found another body. But by now she will be riding north to meet Jacques Fournier."

"Yes, of course. Well, send her the images anyway. She will pick them up later."

"Oh," Clarice said, staring at the screen.

"What is it?"

"There's an order from the SS following the sabotage at Maluanay. Dated 1942. Signed by an Untersturmführer Vogel. Didn't that name crop up somewhere else?"

"He was Richter's deputy in Rouen. Send that to Pascale as well."

"Will do." Clarice tapped out an email outlining Kerr's military history and attached the photographs they had. Pascale could pick them up when she arrived in Brionne.

Millau, Present Day

Georges was sitting outside his modest home, taking in the sunshine. His stick was resting by the chair. On the table was a partly completed jigsaw puzzle. As Patrice approached, walking up the small path to the house, he rose awkwardly.

"Don't rush, Papa," Patrice said. "I'll go inside and put some coffee on."

"I'm not an invalid, Patrice. Valerie called the other day, and she was the same. Bothered and fussed around me like a doctor, not a granddaughter."

"She did say." Patrice smiled at the old man. "You aren't a spring chicken any more, and those bones take time to heal. She was just thinking about your health."

"Humph. I'd like her to kiss me on the cheek and talk about family and friends, not interrogate me like those chumps at the hospital."

"They are not chumps, Papa, they are health professionals."

The old man waved his hand irritably. "Whatever. They thought I was going senile."

Patrice grinned. The old man's body might be frail these days, but his mind was still sharp.

"Well, thankfully, you are not, and we are all glad of it. Now, I brought some pastries. I'll put them on the table here and make coffee. We can catch up out here in the sunshine."

He put his small bag of pastries on the table, paused, and placed a piece on the jigsaw in its place. He winked and went into the house to turn on the coffee maker. He returned a few moments later and poured two cups.

"Valerie's ministrations aside, how are you, Papa?"

"I am well enough. I broke my hip, not my brain."

Patrice laughed and sipped his coffee. "Papa, there was something I wanted to broach with you. You know that Pascale and I are researching her grandmother."

"Valerie said something about that, yes. You're digging up old bones, Patrice. Bones that should be left to rest in peace is my thinking on the matter."

He settled back with his coffee and looked across at his son, sipping it before placing it back on the table. "But you are going to, anyway."

"Literally, as it turns out. They have found some old bones near Pau, and some of those are the people we are investigating."

Georges raised an eyebrow. "Well, that is fascinating."

"I know it's not directly related, but I wondered if you had any memories of that time. You would have been around eleven or twelve, then?"

"Ah, yes." The old man reached for his coffee and took a sip, savouring the bitter flavour on his tongue. "Yes, I remember some things. Maman sometimes talked in English. I do remember that, Hushed words, a sense of urgency, that sort of thing. There were strangers staying, and we children were shooed away and told to keep quiet. I saw a pair of boots outside the cellar door once, and she snatched them away, telling me to forget what I had seen. It is all fragments, I'm afraid. Of course, in this part of France, we didn't have the Boche looking over our shoulders, but the Gendarmerie was in the pockets of the invaders." He spat his contempt that had remained buried for eighty years. "Still, water under the bridge now."

They sat and ate the pastries and drank their coffee in companionable silence for a few moments. "Does any of that help?" Georges said.

Patrice shrugged. "It is an insight, that is all. I wasn't looking for clues in the case. I just wondered what your experience was. We've never talked about it, and I thought maybe we should. Although I suppose this would have been on the route to the Pyrenees."

"I dug up a coin a few months back while digging out the potatoes. Before this," he pointed at his hip. Georges made to stand.

"No, let me," Patrice said.

"In the tin box by the clock. Bring it out."

Patrice went into the house, found an ancient tin biscuit box on the mantlepiece by the clock, and brought it back outside, giving it to his father.

Georges opened it and rummaged around, eventually bringing out his prize, handing it to Patrice, who took it and turned it over in his hand. "An English half-crown dated 1932. A bit of a find, Papa."

"Well, a Frenchman wouldn't have dropped it from his pocket, would he?"

"No, I suppose not."

"Then that probably came from an allied airman making for Spain. This was one of the routes the evaders used going towards the Pyrenees."

"I wonder if he made it," Patrice said, turning the coin over again.

"We will never know," Georges said. He reached for one of the pastries and took a bite "Not every resistance story ended in glory, Patrice. Some ended in silence, and maybe that was for the best."

Chapter 9

Lodève, Present Day

Radfield was first in the office, having flown back the evening before, when he went to Pégairolles and spent a pleasant evening with Laurence.

"How did things go in Berlin?" she said, as Radfield sat down warily and looked at the two dogs, waiting to leap onto his lap. They sat, like two predators, tongues lolling and tails rhythmically thumping the floor, biding their time.

"I made some progress," he said.

Clarice sat on the sofa and looked up as Laurence busied herself cooking the evening meal.

"David put me in touch with the archivist over there, *Maman*."

"And has anything come of it?"

"Well, yes, as a matter of fact, it has. She called me just before I left the office. Now that we know that Kerr was living under his mother's maiden name, Ingrid…"

"Oh, Ingrid now," Radfield said, teasing.

"Yes, Ingrid has found some university records."

"Where?"

"Leipzig."

***

Radfield smiled at the memory as he busied himself starting the coffee machine. Just as it was bubbling away and filling the office with its aroma, he heard the door open. Clarice came in, followed by Patrice.

"David, good flight?" Patrice said.

"Uneventful," he said. "I was followed about in Berlin, but they didn't try anything."

Patrice frowned. "I wonder why?"

Radfield shrugged. "Pascale not back yet, I take it?"

"No. She is going to Rouen, following up on a lead," Patrice said. "Oh, I took the liberty of asking François to come along today. He said he would be here about now. While we are waiting, let's go into Pascale's office and sort out what we have."

Pascale's inner sanctum was littered with notes, maps, and old photographs. A half-empty coffee cup from the day before sat beside Pascale's notebook, and a corkboard on the wall was covered in pinned documents. The early morning light flooded through the window, giving the cluttered office a bright atmosphere. Patrice picked up the documents on the desk and put them in a pile, allowing Radfield some space to put his briefcase.

"Hello, are you there?" François called out from the reception lobby.

"In here, François," Patrice said. He looked about the room. "Bring a chair in with you while you are at it."

François came in carrying one of the lobby chairs and placed it down. "Bit of a squeeze in here," he said.

"Indeed, but we thought it a good idea to keep you informed, François, even if you are officially off the case," Patrice said. "David has just come back from Berlin, so I think that is the first thing on the agenda."

"Berlin was interesting," Radfield said, taking out copies of the documents he had taken in Germany from his briefcase and placing them on the desk. "And frustrating."

"What did you find out?" Patrice said.

"Okay, well, James Kerr attended school in Germany in the 1920s, which is when he vanished from the records in the UK. I found an enrolment at a school in Frankfurt. The enrolment list shows a James Kerr.

"However, I could find nothing following his school records. No university or anything. By that time, the Nazis were starting to come into play. I started wondering if they returned to the UK."

"Since then, Ingrid has been in touch," Clarice said. "James Kerr switched to using his mother's surname, Krüger. She found university records in Leipzig, where he studied history and languages. David's hunch was right, though. Following university, he did go back to Scotland."

"British intelligence files on Kerr show him as an officer in the military in the mid-1930s," Radfield said. "But there is a gap. The gaps are unexplained. I don't know, maybe there's a cover-up."

Patrice grinned. "While you were en route, we managed to fill in some of those gaps. He joined the Royal Scots, but was transferred into SIS in 1938, then vanished off the records, so as you say, we are assuming that's when he was recruited into SOE."

"What did you find in Paris?" François asked Patrice.

"I found no mention of Vanguard beyond Claire's notebook. I've copied it all, what there is of it, so we can go through it properly here and see if it throws anything else up. At the time, the SS were managing affairs in Rouen. What is interesting is that the head of the SS," he paused and looked at his notes, "Obersturmführer Franz Richter, was assassinated by the resistance in early 1943. There is mention of this in Claire's notes. It took place after the attack on the railway. If I were to hazard a guess, the SS were homing in. After the assassination, his second in command, an Untersturmführer Heinrich Vogel, took over..."

"Vogel?" Radfield said.

"Yes," Patrice looked up. What of it?"

Radfield frowned. "I came across that name somewhere." He rummaged through his notes, eventually smiling. "Ah, here it is, a Heinrich Vogel was at the same school as Kerr. They were in the same year."

Patrice sipped his coffee. "So they would have known each other. That would have been dangerous for Kerr."

"I'm sorry to interrupt," Viala said, "but where is this leading us? How does it fit in with what happened to Lucien Defrense?"

Patrice sighed. "I'm sorry, François, but I really don't know at this stage. I just thought it would be helpful to keep you up to date. It might help, it might not."

Viala nodded. "Very well, please, carry on."

"Apparently, Vogel was recalled to Berlin following the July 4 plot against Hitler. The trail goes cold after that," Patrice said.

"If Kerr and Vogel knew each other before the war, then no wonder Kerr took great care to conceal his face when he met Claire. Had she been captured, she would have been tortured," Radfield said.

"How do we know she wasn't?" Clarice had been silent up to this point, but started to think aloud. "What if that is what happened? That would explain her disappearance."

"But according to the files we found, she went to the Pyrenees," Patrice said. "She and three others were escorting allied airmen to Spain."

"Which brings us to Pascale's trip to Pau," Patrice said. "What did she find there?"

"Indeed. They discovered three bodies."

"Four now," Patrice said.

"Yes, that is why Pascale went back. So far we have Anton Marchand, André Fournier and Jean Luc Defrense."

"Aigle, Orage and Mistral," David said. "And one more. Hang on, how many allied airmen were there?"

Patrice paused. "One by the looks of it." He frowned. "Something is off here. Three escorts for one evader." He shook his head. "No, something isn't right here. And if Claire was with them, that's a big escort for one allied airman."

"Yes. But Mistral had been shot. What looked like an execution. There was no evidence of Claire, so we have limited information. Beyond that, there was a murder. The other two deaths are inconclusive, according to Doctor Caron. They think they were shot, but won't be pressed on the matter. I'm not sure how much further forward we are. All of our protagonists are either confirmed dead or missing. I am at a loss now."

"What about this fourth body?" Radfield said.

Clarice shook her head. "So far, no identification."

"And what is Pascale doing now, still in Pau?"

"We found the Fourniers' son. She went to see him in Brionne. I haven't heard back yet."

"What we do have," Patrice said, "are some photographs." He pulled the images from the file and went to the corkboard to pin them up. "We have most of our protagonists on camera, so it gives us something to focus on."

David Radfield watched as he did this. One particular image caught his attention. He froze, staring at it. His eyes widened, and his face drained of colour. He stared at the image, lips parting. "Wait..." He lifted it off the board, stepping back into the light and brought it closer, peering at it. "Oh, my... Oh, my, oh, my. You clever bastard."

Patrice and Clarice exchanged glances. "What is it?" Patrice asked.

"I need to make a phone call. Just a moment."

He walked back to the main office and picked up his phone from where he had left it on Clarice's desk. They heard him talking before he came back into the room.

"Okay, I've just had this sent over from Ingrid," he said.

He put the phone down on the desk, and they looked at it one by one. David scanned the room as they saw what he had just seen.

"Oh, my God," Patrice said. "This changes everything."

Clarice looked at the images side by side. The man they had been tracking had a face. And they were looking at betrayal hidden in plain sight. "*Merde.*"

"I need to go back to London," Radfield said.

***

Brionne, Present Day

Pascale rode across the country from Pau. She eschewed the autoroutes, as the most direct route avoided them. Besides, she thought, this was an excuse for a long, uninterrupted bike ride through France, so she would make the most of it. Riding emptied her mind in much the same manner as meditation.

From Pau, she headed north to Mont-de-Marsan, then northeast towards Brive-la-Gaillard, thence in the general direction of Châteauroux and Blois, passing west of Orléans. When she saw the twin towers of Chartres on the horizon, she knew she was close to her destination. Having navigated the roundabouts of Chartres, she struck north on the N154, through Dreux, Evreux, where she picked up the D613 heading northwest before picking up the D130 to Brionne. By the time she arrived, it was late, so she found an auberge and settled for the night, where she had a meal and settled down for a deep, dreamless sleep that only comes at the end of a long ride. Monsieur Fournier would wait until tomorrow.

***

Pascale found the cottage on the outskirts of Brionne. It was a small stone structure with a large garden. The white shutters were bright and recently painted. The garden was well tended, with red geraniums in pots along the gravelled path and on the steps leading to the front door.

Pascale parked the bike and locked her helmet to it before pushing open the gate with a slight creak and walking along the path, her boots scrunching on the gravel. She could smell lavender in the air and looked across to where the bees were busy working from one tiny flower to the next. The air was alive with the sound of their wings as they went about their task. She lifted the knocker and rapped on the door. Inside, she could hear someone moving about.

"On my way."

Eventually, the door opened, and a man stood there looking at her through round spectacles. His hair was thick and white. Pascale looked at him, taking everything in. Given his age at the time of the war, he would be in his nineties, she thought.

She reached out a hand. "Pascale Hervé, you are expecting me."

The man took her hand, then stepped back, gesturing for her to enter. "Go along the corridor to the kitchen," he said. "I have some coffee on the go. I assume you will join me."

"Yes, please... Artur, or would you prefer Jacques?"

"It's been Artur for so long, my dear, that I can barely remember Jacques. So, yes, Artur, will be fine."

He walked with a sprightly step belying his advanced years and went to the coffee pot on the side where he poured two cups. "Please," he said, "take a seat."

Pascale sat at the wooden table that dominated the kitchen. The window was ajar, and sunlight poured through it, filling the room with light and the scent of the garden outside.

Artur placed a cup on the table in front of Pascale and she took it, wondering how to broach the subject of her visit.

"Did my colleague tell you why I am making enquiries, Monsieur?"

"She did. But I am not sure I will be much help, madame. I was very young at the time, and so many years have passed. Memories fade with time, you know."

"Perhaps start by telling me about your parents."

The old man sighed and leaned back. "Yes, mama and papa. So long, so long. The Boche murdered Mama near the end of the war. They were rounding people up in reprisals as they retreated. But papa, no one knows."

Pascale smiled. Monsieur, I have some news for you."

Artur stiffened. "What?"

"We, well, some archaeologists, have found your father."

"Where?"

"Near Pau. In the mountains. There were several members of a resistance cell in a cave on one of the trails leading to Spain. They have identified all but one of the bodies. One of them is your father. You will be able to bury him now. And when I have finished my investigation, hopefully, I will be able to shed light on what happened to him for you, just as I can for my grandmother."

"So he has been there all this time?"

Pascale nodded. "Yes, monsieur."

Pascale watched as a mix of emotions passed Artur's face. Sadness, relief and loss. His hand trembled slightly as he placed his cup back down on the table. "You must forgive me, madame…"

"There is nothing to forgive," she said. "It will be a shock, I know." The past has a way of catching up, she thought. This man was to finally have closure.

Artur took a deep breath. "How can I help, madame?" he said, breaking her reverie.

"What can you tell me about the time you were living at the Café Lys Noir?"

He shrugged. "As I said, very little that is likely to be of help to you."

"People came and went," she said. "Resistance members, yes?"

"Yes. I remember a young woman. They called her Flamme. She was dark, like you. You look a lot like her, but she was younger. She must have been in her twenties."

Pascale nodded. "Claire Lemoine. She was my *Grand-mère*."

"Ah, yes, I see. Yes, she was a regular there." He frowned. "I do remember a man calling who kept his face hidden by a hat. He often came at the same time."

"They were meeting," Pascale said. "That is the man I am interested in. He was known as Vanguard."

"Ah, yes, yes, I remember that name. Vanguard." He stopped, his brow furrowed as he thought back eighty years. "There was something about him." Again, he paused, and Pascale leaned forward.

"What, Monsieur. What is it that you remember?"

"He was German. I heard him speak it once."

"Yes, we know he spent time in Germany as a child. He spoke it fluently."

Artur shook his head. "No, madame, you misunderstand. I mean, he *was* a German. I saw what looked like a uniform under his coat once."

Pascale sat back and met the man's eyes. "Monsieur, this is important. What type of uniform?"

Artur shook his head and smiled. "Oh, madame, that much I recall very clearly. A dark coat, from what I recall." He shook his head. "It was so long ago. I just remember something about it that looked as if it was German. The collar had insignia on it, but what, exactly, I cannot say."

He stood. "Wait here. I have some papers and things that my mother left. Some of it might be of use to you."

He left the room, and she heard him rummaging about upstairs. She sipped her coffee and looked at the garden outside. It was peaceful in the sunlight, she thought. The neatly tended raised beds of vegetables and the geraniums along the pathways. In that moment, it seemed that the war was a world and a half away, which, she thought to herself, it was. She caught the scent of lavender in the air and turned.

"You know who Vanguard was, don't you?" Geneviève said.

Pascale turned back. Geneviève sat at the table looking at her. "You've worked it out, haven't you?"

"I'm beginning to think I have, yes. I need more, but it is starting to make sense."

She looked past Geneviève as she heard Artur come back along the hall. In that moment, Geneviève was gone.

"Here, some documents and bits and pieces," he said, putting an old box on the table. "Some of it might help."

He opened the box and pulled out bits of paper, now curled and yellowed with age. Receipts and notes. Pascale picked up one of them. "This is a plan for an attack on a railway," she said. "Claire mentioned that in her journal. This confirms it. Oh, what is this?" There were some photographs. She recognised Claire and Jean-Luc.

She looked at Artur. "These are your parents?" She said.

He shook his head and took it from her, holding it up to the light, looking at it as if for the first time. "Yes." He said. "A long time ago, madame. A very long time ago." He stared at it, running his finger gently across it.

"Do you mind if I take these? You will get them all back as soon as we have finished our investigation."

"Of course, madame. About my father. Who should I speak to about getting him back? I want to arrange the funeral, after all."

"Of course, monsieur." She picked up a piece of notepaper lying on the side and wrote Caron's number. "This is Dr Caron, the lead archaeologist. He will put you in touch with the local police. They have been trying to find you anyway, so we have helped them out."

"There is something I do remember," Artur said as she prepared to leave. My parents witnessed something awful. They shooed me back into the back room, where I couldn't see what was going on. Later, I discovered that another resistance cell had been executed en masse in the square.

"Yes," Pascale said. "*La Silhouette*, my assistant found evidence of that. The SS hanged them all."

"Ah, but my Father was convinced they had been betrayed. It was something he said often in the time that followed. That there was a collaborator, but they never found out who it was." He shook his head. "Would that have something to do with what happened in the mountains?"

"I don't know, monsieur." Pascale sat back and pondered. "Claire made subtle hints about that in her journal. She was sure there was faulty intelligence when they sabotaged the railway at Malaunay. They were supposed to be attacking a troop train." She paused, pressing her lips together as she thought.

"I have an idea, Monsieur. A hunch, if you like." A hunch, but maybe one that could lead to a reckoning.

"What is that?"

Pascale smiled, picked up her phone, and dialled.

"Clarice, how are things going?"

"Very well, madame, we are making progress here. Do you have news?"

"I am with Artur Giraud. He raised the issue of betrayal. We have been picking up vague hints. A neighbouring cell was rounded up and executed."

"*La Silhouette*, yes."

"I think you may have uncovered a significant clue with that."

"Thank you, madame."

"I want you to follow that one up. Specifically, I want you to look for someone who had close links with both cells. Find that person, and I think we may have our collaborator. If you don't find what you are looking for online, then go to Paris."

"Oh, a trip to Paris would be nice."

"It's not a joyride, Clarice."

She heard Clarice laughing as she hung up.

Monsieur," she said, meeting his gaze. "I think we may uncover some secrets that would lay your parents to rest."

"That would be good, madame. Perhaps the truth will bring a sense of peace."

"Time I was going, Monsieur. I've taken up enough of your valuable time as it is." She put on her jacket and they went outside.

She was walking with him to the bike when he paused. "You know it is still there, madame?"

"What?"

"The Café Lys Noir. They turned it into a resistance museum. They might be able to help you."

***

Lodève, Present Day

Following the meeting, Clarice sat down alongside Patrice as they worked through the files and snippets they had already, piecing together timelines and people. Clarice brought her laptop into Pascale's office, which was now serving as a de facto conference room. With the sun streaming in through the windows, the place had an airy feel to it as summer sweltered outside.

"Clarice," Patrice said. "See if you can find anything related to that last escape run south in the resistance records. Maybe something to do with who went? In the meantime, I need to pop out to the Carrefour, we are running low on coffee, milk and sugar."

"Very good, monsieur, but get some biscuits, too, we are nearly out of those." Patrice grinned and went out, leaving her alone. Radfield had taken a much-needed day off and was spending it with Laurence, walking the dogs at La Couvertoirade.

Later, Patrice came back, and Clarice looked up as he came into the room. "Monsieur, the Resistance records have a notebook with Anton Marchand's messages. Most of them are of no help, or we already know the circumstances, but there is one about the run to the Pyrenees." She turned the laptop and showed him the screen. "Look. 'Acknowledged Vanguard cover compromised STOP. Immediate Extract Vanguard authorised STOP.' As it is not Claire, I suspect that fourth body might be him."

Patrice nodded. "Send Pascale that information. She's still in Rouen, so hopefully she will pick it up before she gets back."

Chapter 10

Mercerie Dupont, Rue Saint-Sever, Rouen, 1943

Eddie Hargrove and Charlie Sinclair had been waiting for several days. Claire had left them with strict instructions to remain as quiet as possible and not to allow anyone from outside to see them, having concealed them in the attic.

Then she left them. Twice a day, someone came to feed them. He said little other than to introduce himself as Mistral. He dropped off bread, cheese and water. Sometimes, there was a little meat, but that was in pitifully small proportions, and once every other day. "Rationing," Mistral explained. "We share what we can."

"How long are they going to keep us in this hole?" Eddie said as he chewed on the bread. "And these frogs need to learn how to make bread. And while I'm complaining, their coffee is pretty awful, too. No offence to our hosts."

Charlie grinned. "No plans for holidays in France when this lot blows over, then, Flight?"

"Humph! We just need to get out and back to our squadron. Jerry still needs a bloody nose before we talk about holidays."

Mistral called one evening, carrying a satchel and a larger back pack, and handed each of them a pack of papers. "Identity documents and travel passes," he said.

"Monsieur Hargrove," he said, handing Eddie his documents. "You are Marcel Dubois. You are a farmhand, born in Caen in 1915. You are travelling to Bordeaux as a seasonal worker. You have limited education, so you will avoid speaking. Allow Monsieur Sinclair to answer any questions the sentries might ask at checkpoints, *d'accord*?"

Eddie nodded.

"Your wife was killed during the bombing in 1940. You have no fixed address, so you are itinerant." He turned to Charlie, "Monsieur has suffered a throat injury during the bombing, so he says little, preferably nothing at all. Any questions, he defers to you, understand?"

"Got it, old chap. My French is pretty good, having spent plenty of holidays here before the war."

"I noticed. You have a southern accent. Where did you stay?"

"Little place in Provence. When this lot is over, I want to go and live down that way."

"I prefer Blackpool, at least you get English grub," Eddie said with a grunt.

Charlie ignored the interruption and lapsed into silence, sensing that Mistral had more to say.

"Monsieur Hargrove, this is your *Carte d'identité* issued in Caen showing you are an *ouvrier Agricole*. This is the German *Ausweis* permitting travel from here to Bordeaux, valid for one month. This is your work permit for Château Laroche, requesting your presence for work, and this is your Vichy ration card. *D'accord?*"

"*D'accord,*" Eddie said, ignoring Mistral's wince at his accent.

"Monsieur, please, whatever you do, remain silent. The Bosche will pick you up immediately if you talk, so don't."

He opened up the backpack and took out some old, worn clothes. "Put these on." He handed Eddie a threadbare jacket with patches at the elbows, a flat cap and worn trousers, ignoring Eddie's wrinkled nose at their state. "Your boots will pass as workmen's boots," he said.

He turned to Charlie. "You are Paul Lefèvre, a textile merchant based here in Rouen. Don't worry about your accent, the Bosche won't realise it isn't local. It is good enough for our purposes. Your *carte d'Identié* issued here in Rouen. You were born in 1918 and are unmarried. You are travelling to Toulon to negotiate a contract with Vichy-approved factories. I have some samples of cloth for you to carry with you. Here is your *Ausweis*. Here is a business letter from Maison Textile Rouen, and finally, your Vichy-issued ration card and travel voucher."

"Jolly good," Charlie said, taking the documents. "What do I get to wear?"

Mistral took a business suit from the pack and handed it over. It was a lightly worn, grey double-breasted affair accompanied by a fedora hat and a pair of worn but still smart, polished shoes.

"Well, that's a whole lot smarter than me," Eddie said.

Charlie grinned. "Should have paid attention during your French lessons at school, Flight."

"Humph."

"I will be back tomorrow," Mistral said, checking his watch and pausing briefly at the top of the steps. With that, he was gone.

As Mistral left, Charlie frowned. "Odd sort of chap," he said.

"He's French," Eddie said, stretching out. "They're all odd."

Charlie let it go. "Yes, maybe you are right."

***

Two streets away, in a van parked in a side alleyway out of sight of the property, SS-Oberscharführer Klaus Weber, the radio operator, took off his headset and gestured to the Untersturmführer Vogel, who was standing by. "Well, Herr Untersturmführer? Do we round them up?"

Vogel smiled. "No, Oberscharführer, that would give the game away. Be patient. Let them run. We can catch them at Gare de Rouen-Rive-Droite. That way, it will look more natural, and we can keep the safe house under surveillance."

Weber frowned and Vogel grinned as he opened his cigarette case and took out a cigarette. "You need to learn the art of the long game, Herr Oberscharführer."

"If you say so, Herr Untersturmführer."

"Oh, I do. I do indeed."

***

Upper Floor of Café Lys Noir, Rouen, 1943

Claire looked around the room at her compatriots. They weren't happy. The room was dimly lit, with the blackout curtains containing what little light there was from outside, and the air was thick with smoke from cigarettes. She could hear the pitter-patter of the rain tapping against the window, muting the sounds of the city below. She wondered if it would ever stop. Three of them were gathered around a worn wooden table. The other two listened intently as she laid out the plan she had agreed with Vanguard.

"Have you heard from Jean-Luc?" Suzanne Moreau said.

Claire shook her head. "No. He's at Mercerie Dupont. He is taking the two Mosquito crewmen who came down last month to Spain, so he will be gone for a while. It was time to move them south anyway."

"So he won't be involved in this?"

"No. By the time he gets back, the plans will be too far advanced to bring him up to date. He can sit this one out."

"Agreed," André Fournier said, drawing on his cigarette. "But why are we planning this anyway?" None of us has met this Vanguard character apart from you and, well, Marguerite briefly as he comes and goes. Now he wants us to carry out what could be a very dangerous mission and may well put the whole cell in danger. The repercussions will be brutal. Remember *La Silhouettes*. Hanging in the town square is not something I relish."

"Yes, my thoughts, too," Suzanne said. She looked about the room and fixed her stare on Claire. "None of us wants Richter here, but he is the devil we know, and he is an administrator. It's the Gestapo we need to worry about."

Claire sat back, thinking briefly about her run-in with Klaus Falkenrath. The man had put her on edge. He was watching, and she wasn't convinced he would take her brush-off at face value. The rest of the cell was asking precisely the questions she had expected them to ask. The questions she was asking herself.

***

The Previous Evening

As usual, the room had been in darkness when she met Vanguard the previous evening.

"Richter is travelling to Berlin next week," he said. "I cannot allow him to go."

"Why?"

He reached for his cigarette case, drew out a tube, and lit it. The flare briefly lit the contours of his face. In the shadows, she saw the slightest shake of his head.

"My cover is at risk. That's all you need to know. If he gets to Berlin, people die. Not just you and your cell."

He placed a dossier on the table. She didn't reach for it. There would be time to read it later.

"And the risk to us?" she said. "The reprisals that will follow? It's one thing to sabotage rail lines or power stations. We lost a whole cell following the assassinations of low-ranking Wehrmacht officers. What do you think will happen after this? To assassinate the senior SS officer in Rouen? That will bring hell down on our heads. What does Spencer say?"

"Spencer is fine with it. He understands the necessity."

She leaned back and exhaled sharply. "Ordinary people will pay the price for this."

"It's war. There are casualties in war. We need to win. Richter is an obstacle. He must be removed."

Silence stretched between them, and he smoked without looking her way, peering through a small gap in the blackout curtain to the street below. She wondered what he saw that was so fascinating, but didn't ask.

"I'm not happy about this," she said at last. "Neither will the others be, when I tell them."

"I don't need your happiness. I need your compliance."

He stood and walked to the door.

"Who is A.K.?" she asked.

He paused, hand on the doorframe. "What?"

"A.K. The initials on your cigarette case. I noticed. I wondered."

He turned the handle. "Old gift," he said.

***

Frankfurt 1932

Otto Reinhardt watched as James Kerr walked across the playing fields toward him. He lifted a hand in greeting, and James acknowledged it with a smile. "Hello, Otto."

It seemed to James that the man had aged much since they first met, eleven years previously. He'd lost some of his stiffness, and he had adopted a slight stoop these days, his frame weighed down by time and a persistent cough. Meanwhile, James was a young man growing into maturity, his sandy hair catching the late afternoon light.

As James got closer, Reinhardt pulled out his cigarette case and flipped it open, offering one to the young man, who took it. They both lit up and stood for a short while, enjoying the moment of companionship, the faint shouts and thuds of boys kicking a ball carrying on the still air.

"I hear congratulations are in order," Reinhardt said. "Leipzig, studying languages. I am proud of you, boy. I am very proud. Your father would be too, I don't doubt."

"It's a good placement, Otto."

"How is your mother these days?"

"Her health isn't so good, but she manages."

"I'm sorry to hear that, but mine isn't so good either. This cough is getting worse. Still, with young men like you, the future is assured." He paused and looked across the playing fields, where the boys' laughter mingled with the dull thud of the ball and a cheer as it went into the goalmouth. "There are great changes coming," he said. "Germany is rising from the ashes. You can hear it in the rallies in Munich, the new voices shaping our future."

"I know."

Reinhardt stood, smoking and looking into the distance. "You won't see so much of me when you are in Leipzig. We will keep in touch, though."

"I will miss you, Otto. You have been a good friend to my mother and me."

Reinhardt nodded, took the cigarette case out of his pocket, and held it out. "I want you to have this, boy. It's a reminder of what we've built, and what you'll carry forward. Think of me."

"I can't, really, Otto. It was a gift from your wife."

"And now it is a gift from me to you. Please take it. I insist."

James took the proffered case, his fingers tracing the "A.K." engraving. He felt a surge of gratitude for Otto, who had given him a new life, but also a flicker of unease at the "rise" Otto spoke of, a future he couldn't yet see, his grip tightening briefly on the case. "*Alles klar*, eh, Otto?"

"Yes, *alles klar*, James. It's what we always say in the *Kulturverein. R*eady for what's next. *Alles klar.*"

James looked down at the case and ran his fingers over the engraving, A.K., the silver glinting in the fading sunlight.

***

Vanguard's fingers played along the engraving, worn now with age, as he pondered Claire's interest. He looked back at her. "Wondering can get you killed," he said. Then he laughed softly, almost kindly, his gaze lingering on the case for a moment. "*Alles klar*. It was a gift. From someone. Long gone now."

Claire's jaw tightened, her eyes narrowing slightly, but she nodded.

He opened the door, the case slipping into his pocket with a faint glint. "Now, just get the job done, eh?"

***

The Following Evening, Café Lys Noir

She placed the folder on the table that Vanguard had given her the evening before. "If it helps."

Fournier picked it up and leafed through the contents. "Richter thinks there has been infiltration in the SS? Where did this come from?" He peered at the documents. "They seem genuine. So what if they do think that? They can squabble among themselves and leave us alone for a while. It has nothing to do with us."

"Vanguard says his cover is at risk."

"So we risk French lives in the inevitable reprisals to save one agent?"

"That's one way of looking at it," Claire said. "But if he is caught, then the repercussions will cost French lives anyway, so whatever we do, there is a risk. Last night, he told me that we are all at risk if Richter lives."

"You trust this man?" Fournier said.

"He's SOE, as am I, so yes. As much as you can trust anyone these days."

"And your contact in London?"

"I have to speak to him. We need authorisation. Vanguard tells me that he has already approved the mission."

Suzanne nodded. "Then we do it."

Fournier grunted and lit a cigarette. "So how are we going to do this? A sniper?"

Suzanne sipped her coffee. "And who here is a good enough shot for that? I'm not."

They all looked at each other. Their silence answered the question.

"Then we set up an ambush," Fournier said. "We hijack a vehicle, block the road, and one of us gets close enough to take the kill shot." He glanced at Claire. "I can handle the vehicle. Anton and I will take care of that. You focus on the kill shot."

She had expected this. She was the one who brought the mission, so it was inevitable that they would expect her to do the dirty work. She nodded.

"Yes, of course." She put a map of the city on the table. "This is the route he will take to the chateau where he is meeting other SS officers for a conference before going to Berlin. He is planning to travel next Thursday." She looked up at Fournier. "Make your plans to have a vehicle." She pointed at the map. "Here. Where the road narrows and there is a slight bend, so that his driver will see the truck too late to be able to respond, is, I think, the best place for an ambush. Also, we can make our own getaway before anyone can raise the alarm. We will need to all separate and meet back here later. *D'accord?*"

There were nods of agreement. "*D'accord,*" Fournier said. "And *Bonne chance.*"

***

Rouen, 1943

Vogel watched as Richter sat in the back of the staff car. "I will be back later this afternoon," Richter said.

Vogel clicked his heels and gave a salute. "Heil Hitler." As Richter's car pulled away, a faint smirk played across Vogel's lips. He had other things to be doing.

Richter raised an arm in response and gestured to the driver. "Drive on, sergeant."

The man selected first gear and drove off through the streets of Rouen, heading out into the open countryside to the chateau where Richter was planning to meet other high-ranking SS officers. As they headed out of the city, Richter relaxed and sat back, smoking a cigarette, looking idly out at the flat landscape of northern France.

Further to the east, where the road narrowed and stone walls separated the road from the fields, Fournier and Anton waited. A few hours earlier, they had stolen a delivery truck and were now waiting at the roadside with the bonnet up, feigning a breakdown. Fournier sat in the driving seat, tapping the wheel as he waited.

Anton stood at the front with his head below the bonnet, looking back along the road.

"Here he is," he said.

Fournier started the engine and kept it running, ready. Anton kept his eyes on the staff car as it drew closer. He looked across at the gateway opposite, where Claire waited. Her heart was beating faster now as the moment drew closer. The staff car came to a stop, unable to pass through the narrow gap. The driver called out.

"Move that thing, quickly now!"

Anton stepped out from the shelter of the bonnet. "I'm sorry, we have broken down. We cannot move."

The sergeant grumbled and stepped out. "Here, let me see to it."

As he walked across to the truck, Claire stepped out from behind the gateway, Vanguard's dossier flashing in her mind. It was the perfect spot for an ambush. He'd been right. In two strides, she was across the road, pistol raised. As her grip tightened, Spencer's words echoed in her mind: "*Make the occupation as difficult as possible.*" Then those of McTaggart, the crusty Chief Petty Officer, "*if you are going to point a gun at someone, then you shoot to kill, before they kill you.*" She couldn't hesitate. Not now, but there was a brief intake of breath before she shot the man in the throat. As he fell back, Richter stood in the back of the staff car, his hand fumbling for his sidearm, but before he could draw, Claire fired again, putting a bullet through his temple. His body staggered back and crumpled into the seat.

"Quickly," she said.

The other two scrambled down to the car. They lifted the bodies into the back of the truck. Fournier poured petrol over the Mercedes and set light to it. As they drove off, there was a loud 'whump' as the fire ignited the fuel tank, and Fournier could see a black plume of smoke rising in the sky.

Claire stared straight ahead. Two deaths. Two clean shots. Two men she had looked in the eye before pulling the trigger. What had she become?

Gare de Rouen-Rive-Droite, 1943

Eddie Hargrove and Charlie Sinclair walked ahead of Mistral, who lingered a few paces behind, scanning the crowds on the approach to the station. No one paid them any attention, and they walked separately to avoid the appearance of travelling together.

As they approached the checkpoint, they could see the Wehrmacht soldiers, Kar98ks slung over their shoulders. They had a bored competence about them as they flicked their eyes over the documents and back up at the owners, checking for likenesses, before offering a curt *'guten tag'* and gesturing the traveller through. Nearby, an SS Untersturmführer lounged, smoking a cigarette.

"Vogel," Mistral said in a whisper.

"Problem?" Charlie said.

"Don't know. Act naturally, if he doesn't notice, we should be fine."

They joined the queue and waited, shuffling forward until Eddie reached the front. He handed over the papers and stood, forcing himself to meet the soldier's eyes. He risked a brief glance back over his shoulder at Mistral, who shook his head almost imperceptibly. *For god's sake, be natural, you'll get us all caught.*

The sentry paused as he looked up and across at Vogel, inclining his head with a subtle nod. Vogel stiffened, flicked away the remains of his cigarette and strolled over to the checkpoint.

Sweat began to bead on Eddie's brow, and he remained silent, waiting to see what happened.

The sentry handed the papers to Vogel, who scrutinised them. He looked directly at the two airmen.

"Very good," he said in English. "Very good indeed, I commend your artist. However, these... these are forgeries. He turned to Eddie, "Flight Lieutenant Hargrove, I believe, and this must be Flying Officer Sinclair."

"Shit," Eddie said, his shoulders slumping. The sentries snapped to attention, raising their rifles, the bolt actions clicking as one, and Vogel called across to other soldiers. "Take these two away." He turned back to the airmen. "Don't worry, we will take care of you, we are not savages, you know. But, for you two," he paused as if enjoying the moment. "The war is over, yes?"

Mistral melted into the crowd and watched as his two charges were marched away and bundled into the back of a Wehrmacht truck and driven off.

"*Merde!*"

***

Café Lys Noir, Rouen, 1943

What happened?" Claire said.

Jean-Luc shrugged his shoulders. "I have no idea. They were arrested at the station. I slipped away before they could connect me. What else could I have done, madame?"

"Sensible," she said. "Bad enough to lose our charges, but losing one of our own would be devastating. You know too much. We would all be compromised. As it is, we have to assume that the safe house is compromised. We cannot use it again."

"They won't torture Allied airmen, surely? They'll give name, rank, and serial number, nothing more," Jean-Luc said.

"Don't underestimate the Bosche. However, there is something that worries me. You said that Vogel referred to them by name. That means they knew who they were before the checkpoint."

She drummed her fingers on the table. She looked at André. "André, you and I will go to Mercerie Dupont tomorrow."

Fournier frowned. "What have you in mind?"

"A hunch. I want to check it out."

***

Early the following morning, Claire and Fournier cycled through the quiet streets to Mercerie Dupont. They placed the bikes outside and went in. Deserted since Hargrove and Sinclair left, it was in darkness with the shutters closed and the lights off, and dust hung in the air.

"What are we looking for?" Fournier said.

Claire lifted a finger to her lips and shook her head. "We will tidy the place up a little for our next arrivals," she said aloud. "Aigle, you check upstairs and clean the rooms."

She gestured for him to remain, and he nodded. She walked about the room, under tables and behind an old picture that hung on the wall. Then she gestured for Fournier to fetch one of the wooden chairs. Placing it in the middle of the room soundlessly, she stood on it and looked up at the light fitting. Carefully, she unscrewed it. She stopped and looked down at Fournier, gesturing to the fitting. Screwing his eyes, he could see where she was pointing. Inside was a small black disc. She returned the fitting and stepped down from the chair, gesturing to the front door. Once outside, she said. "That's how they knew their names. The place is bugged."

"*Merde*! How did you know?"

"Vogel knew their names. They were only here one night. No one outside the cell knew their identities. So either someone talked, or someone was listening."

Fournier paused as he considered the implications. "Do you think there was anything Jean-Luc could have done differently at the station, Claire?"

She thought about it for a moment and looked at him. *So he thought it off, too.* "With Vogel there, he could have aborted. He should have smelled something was off, but I'm not sure he thinks that way." She shrugged. "What is done is done. The airmen will be POWs, and we have to carry on. I will have a word with Jean-Luc tomorrow. Next time, call it off."

"So now what?"

She walked over to the bicycle. "I need to think. There are two options here. One, abandon the safe house..."

"Or two?"

She grinned. "Or two, play the Bosche at their own game. We use the house to feed the bastards false information."

"But they will arrest us. We took a risk coming here."

"No, I don't think so. They are using this for intelligence gathering. If they wanted to arrest us, they could have done so. They didn't, so we need to think about it."

"We need to tell the others."

"Of course," she said. "Tonight."

Chapter 11

The Café Lys Noir, Present day.

In the back streets of Rouen, now a bustling city that showed little of the dark period of eighty years previously, the Café Lys Noir remained a small oasis of the 1940s, with period advertisements on the walls and original furnishing and decor, its creaking wooden stairs whispering secrets of the past. Pascale parked the bike outside and walked in. The rumble from the engine echoed as it settled into silence.

A woman sat at the bar, reading a paper and looked up as she came in.

"Madame?"

"Bonjour, madame, I called earlier. Pascale Hervé."

"Yes, of course, I'm Madeleine Béraud. It was I that you spoke to. How may I help?"

"Can you please show me the upstairs room where the resistance held their meetings?"

"*Bien sûr*, follow me."

Madeleine led her upstairs. Now that Pascale saw it in real life, the room seemed so tiny. On the walls were pictures, some of which were duplicates of those she had already seen.

"Would you like to see a copy of Flamme's journal, madame?"

"I have seen some parts from the resistance archive."

"This is the full journal. You can look through it if you wish."

She placed the document on the table, and Pascale leafed through it. Some, she had read before: the first meeting with Vanguard and the destruction of the train at Malaunay. She carried on reading through the tersely written entries. "Ah, this I haven't seen." She frowned.

"We killed Richter today. Vanguard's plan. What game is he playing? That SS ring on his finger, the 'A.K.' case. Something's not right. Three of us. Aigle, Orage, and me. Aigle and Orage stole a truck. Used it to block the road. I shot the target and his driver. Disposed of the bodies. Burned the car.

"Strange. No reprisals. We expected reprisals. But nothing. Vogel has taken charge of the SS in Rouen. But all silent. Nothing."

Pascale's frown deepened. No reprisals. That was odd. Why?

A little further on, another entry. Just one line.

"Vogel appointed Obersturmführer in charge of Rouen office."

Further on, another entry. A pair of Allied aircrew had been captured.

"SS have been monitoring safe house at Mercerie Dupont. Place is bugged. May be able to use it for our own purposes, but they know about us. Gestapo have been paying attention. Falkenrath has been watching, but not said anything more. Why didn't Jean-Luc abort?"

Pascale stood. Something was off here. Like Claire before her, the SS's lack of reaction after Richter's assassination puzzled her. She walked around the room, deep in thought, as she looked at the old photographs, one of the burned-out staff car where Richter had met his end.

On one wall was a case with a glass front. She walked over and looked at it. It was a paper napkin, stained with what could have been wine or coffee, with the words "upstairs, alone," written in a neat hand.

"What would this have been?"

"I suppose it might have been used to tell someone about a meeting upstairs. There's a faint 'Flamme, '43' in the corner, but I don't know the full context, madame. I'm sorry," Madeleine said

Pascale looked closely at the napkin, as something triggered in her mind. Frowning, she fished in her phone and found the message Clarice had sent. Holding the image next to the napkin, she could see clearly that the writing was identical.

"Oh, my, it was you all along."

"May I ask?" Madeleine said, interrupting her thoughts. "What is your interest in Claire Lemoine?"

"She was my grandmother. I was told as a child that she vanished during the war. Now I discover that she had a career as a resistance fighter."

Madeline frowned. "Er, it may be nothing..."

"What?"

"Well, there is a letter. It was with the journal when it arrived here near the end of the war."

"Go on?"

"Well, does the name Colette mean anything to you?"

"My mother."

"Wait here." Madeleine disappeared downstairs, came back up with an old envelope, and handed it to Pascale.

"It hasn't been opened," Pascale said.

"No," Madeleine shook her head. "It was kept here for Colette. We couldn't find her, so it has remained here in case she ever came by. Or someone who knew her."

Pascale turned the envelope over in her hands, the paper yellowed with age.

"Can you take it to her?"

"Oh, yes, of course, I can." Pascale struggled to focus on the clear handwriting as her eyes filled up. *Oh, Grand-mère.*

***

National Archives, Kew. Present Day.

Radfield stepped through the main entrance and approached the reception desk. Yvonne Saunders looked up. Something like embarrassment flickered across the eyes, but Radfield disarmed it with a half-smile.

"Inspector Radfield. I didn't expect to see you again. What can I help you with?"

"I need military records. SOE files, and anything from SIS before them. Also, anything on German cultural organisations operating in Britain between the wars."

"Very good. If you'll follow me."

She led him back to the same research office he'd used before. A few minutes later, she returned with a stack of documents and microfiches, placing them on the table. She turned to leave.

"Yvonne," Radfield said, stopping her. "I may call you Yvonne?"

She nodded. "Of course."

"When you make your phone call... tell the man on the other end to come in and join me."

She froze, her smile faltering. "Oh, er, I..."

Radfield gave her a knowing grin. "Yes. I worked it out. I'm a detective, remember?"

Without another word, Yvonne turned and walked briskly back to her desk.

Radfield was busy working through the files when he sensed a presence. He looked up with a raised eyebrow, taking in the man before him. Middle-aged, greying at the temples, immaculately dressed, the sort who could vanish in a crowd.

"MI6?" he asked.

The man sat. "Geoffrey Spencer. Section officer, historical records."

Radfield raised an eyebrow. "Any relation to Arthur?"

Spencer smiled. "My grandfather. I joined the family business, as it were."

Radfield grunted. "Does the family business include murder and attempted murder?"

"Ah. Sorry about that. Our French friends in the DGSI were a little, shall we say, enthusiastic. They felt Monsieur Defrense posed a threat, digging too deeply. They weren't to know he was about to have a heart attack."

Radfield grunted. "To their credit, they appeared to have tried to help."

Spencer nodded. "They did, but the man died instantly. Nothing anyone could have done, as the post-mortem discovered." He shrugged. "It was still untidy."

"And us? That stunt outside? You tried to kill me and my partner."

Spencer gave a small shrug. "No plans to kill you. Just... persuade you to back off."

"Worked out well, that, didn't it?"

Spencer sighed. "Yes, we gathered that. You people are remarkably tenacious. Still, we're asking again. Step away from this."

"Why?"

"Some secrets are best left unexhumed. For everyone's sake."

"And if we don't? Are we doing anything illegal? Threatening national security?"

"Well, no..."

"Are we at risk of exposing something that threatens national security?"

"No. Not security. Not exactly."

"Then what?"

Spencer leaned back in his chair. "How can I put this... What you may uncover would be, well, how can I put this... not in the national interest."

"And if we keep digging?"

Silence.

"I thought so," Radfield said. "There's nothing you can do, short of assassinating us. And I suspect that would raise more questions than it buries." He leaned back, matching Spencer's posture. "I can just see the headlines now. It would make the Spycatcher affair look like a walk in the park."

Spencer flinched at the reference to Spycatcher, then gave a slow nod, conceding the point. "Well, Inspector, let me leave you with this: not everyone you've identified is who they say they are. And nothing, *nothing*, is quite as it appears."

With that, he rose and walked out. Then he paused and turned. "Do you think we like this? Watching old ghosts we have spent decades keeping buried, clawing their way back into the daylight?" He sighed and turned away again, walking out as Radfield watched him go, narrowing his eyes. Something in Spencer's tone. Something in the look he gave. Maybe, just maybe, he wasn't the enemy after all.

He picked up his phone.

"David," Patrice said on the other end.

"Patrice, I think we can stop worrying about the intelligence services. For a while, at least."

***

85 Albert Embankment, London, Present Day (2025)

Geoffrey Spencer strode through the open-plan office on the fifth floor of MI6 headquarters, unbuttoning his coat as he passed rows of desks where analysts quietly interrogated their computers. The hum of activity was a familiar backdrop, but his mind was elsewhere, replaying the tense encounter with David Radfield at the National Archives. Maggie Blunt turned as he approached her desk. She stood to face him, her posture attentive, sensing the weight of his mood.

"Hello, sir," she said, her voice professional but warm. "How did it go?"

"Come into my office, Maggie," Spencer said, smiling slightly on seeing her.

She followed him into his corner office, the door closing behind them with a soft click. The room was sparse but functional, with a view of the Thames shimmering through the tinted glass. "Please, take a seat," Spencer said, gesturing to the chair across from his desk.

Maggie sat, crossing her legs as Spencer walked around his desk and settled into his chair. He took a moment to study her, noting the quiet confidence that had propelled her through the ranks to lead a team of field agents. In her mid-thirties now, she had the same intensity he'd recognised in his grandfather's notes on Claire Lemoine decades ago. A comparison that stirred a flicker of unease as he considered the investigation at hand.

"How did it go, eh?" Spencer began, answering her earlier question with a sigh. "Mixed. Pascale Hervé and her team are pretty determined, and Radfield is like a dog with a bone. He's ex-plod, so that figures. He isn't letting go. Not that I really expected him to. He was recognised as a tenacious operator in the Avon and Somerset Constabulary. Had a good record for catching his man."

"Can you stop them, sir?" Maggie asked, her brow furrowing slightly.

He shook his head, a rueful expression crossing his face. "There's the problem. We cannot get overly enthusiastic like our French colleagues. It took a little diplomacy to calm things down. The French police are very unhappy after the unfortunate demise of Lucien Defrense. Given that, I've told Radfield he can continue."

Maggie leaned forward, her curiosity piqued. "I'm sorry, sir, but I don't understand why we're stopping them anyway. It's all ancient history. What could they uncover that would be a problem for us?"

Spencer sighed again, sitting back in his chair, his fingers steepled in thought. "Maybe nothing. If so, no problem. But some secrets are best kept buried, and we'd prefer they don't see sunlight."

"Those being?" Maggie pressed, her tone respectful but probing.

He shook his head, tapping the side of his nose with a wry smile. "Need to know, Maggie. Need to know."

She nodded, accepting the boundary with a professional ease, though her mind clearly churned with questions. "Then what?"

"I want you to keep your team on it," Spencer said, his voice firm. "But for God's sake, tell them to up their game. Radfield can spot a tail from a mile off."

"And if they do uncover these secrets?" Maggie asked, her expression sharpening.

"If it gets out," Spencer said, voice flat, "Philby will look like a masterclass in damage control."

Maggie's eyes widened slightly. "Oh, that bad?"

"Yes," Spencer confirmed, his jaw tightening. "However, I have a plan. An ace up my sleeve, as it were. So, in the meantime, conduct discreet surveillance and let me know if they find anything troubling. Then I'll put my plan into action."

Maggie stood, smoothing her blazer with a nod. "Straight away, sir. Do we want the French to put surveillance on Hervé's office phone?"

"Yes, do that. It will give us an edge if we need it. Speak to the French and get them on the case."

As she turned to leave, Spencer's gaze lingered on her retreating figure, his thoughts drifting to the secrets buried in SOE's past. Secrets that tied Vanguard's dual identity to a web of wartime betrayals MI6 could ill afford to have exposed. He only hoped his contingency plan would be enough to keep the truth in the shadows, and if it didn't, then decades of silence would unravel, and history would judge them all..

As she reached the door, Maggie paused with her hand on the handle, sensing he wasn't finished.

"Sir?"

Spencer exhaled and swivelled his chair slightly, eyes settling on the sliver of London sky beyond the glass. "There's one more thing," he said. "If Radfield and Hervé push too far, I'll be forced to act."

Maggie turned, frowning. "Forced to act how?"

"There's that ace I can play. But only once."

"A warning?"

Spencer shook his head and smiled. "Let's call it... resolution, on our terms." He tapped his fingers on the desk. It was an insurance policy for when all else failed.

Maggie stepped back outside and paused. *If it's all ancient history, why are we still covering it up?* She shook her head. Such questions didn't help.

***

Paris Gare de Lyon, Present Day

Clarice stepped off the TGV and out into the station concourse. She stepped into the bright Paris morning, clutching her laptop bag as she headed for the cab rank. She took a cab. "*Archives Nationales,*" she said.

"*D'accord* madame."

Once at the archives, she asked for the resistance records and started running cross-references between the cell groups La Liberation and La Silhouette. It didn't take her too long to find what she was looking for, so she picked up the phone.

"*Âllo*, madame."

"*Âllo*," Pascale said. "Where are you at the moment?"

"The *Archives Nationales.*"

"I am presuming that your call is to tell me my hunch paid off?"

"Yes, madame. One man acted as a courier, taking allied airmen to Spain for both groups, but was not executed when *La Silhouettes* were rounded up."

Pascale took a deep breath. "Excellent work, Clarice. We have found our mole."

"Do I get to spend a day sightseeing now?"

Pascale laughed. "Why not? You have earned it. I will see you when you get back."

***

Rouen, Present Day

Pascale decided to stay overnight in Rouen after her visit to the Café Lys Noir. If she set out early the following morning fully rested, she could ride to Lodève in one go rather than stopping partway.

At eight sharp the following morning, she was on the road, leaving Rouen after a good night's sleep. She retraced her route from two days earlier, heading south through Chartres and Orléans, where she picked up the A71. Once on the autoroute, she maintained a steady 130 km/h, stopping only briefly for fuel and comfort. At Clermont-Ferrand, she merged onto the A75, which ran to the coast at Montpellier. She arrived at Lodève late in the afternoon and headed directly for home, rather than calling in at the office. She could catch up with the others tomorrow. An all-day ride was tiring, and she needed a bath and a rest.

The house was quiet and still warm from the afternoon sun. She parked the bike in the garage and stepped into the hallway. She kicked off her boots and rubbed her neck, which ached after a long day in the saddle. Riding was a pleasure, even a long haul on the autoroute, but her neck and back always ached afterwards. She entered the front room, pouring herself a glass of wine just as her phone buzzed with a new email. It was from her estate agent. A potential buyer had made an offer on her old flat. She frowned. It was lower than she would have liked. She dialled the agent.

"Pascale, how are you?"

"Tired, Paul, I've just arrived home from Rouen. Long story. I see you've had an offer."

"I'm sorry, it's lower than we had hoped. I can decline it if you like and hold out for more."

Pascale shook her head. "No, Paul. Accept the offer. I want this done as quickly as possible."

"*D'accord*, Pascale. I'll arrange a meeting with you and the buyer to finalise details, sign the agreement and take a deposit. One day next week?"

"Yes, that should be good."

She hung up and sighed. She thought she could smell the faint odour of lavender. The scent Geneviève used to wear mingled with the faint odour of sandalwood, and she looked around. Geneviève was already seated on the sofa, watching her with quiet interest.

"Good news, then?"

Pascale sighed and sipped her wine. "Mixed."

Geneviève cocked her head in unspoken question.

"The flat is my last link to Guillaume."

"And when that is gone, *chérie*, what then?"

Pascale shrugged. "It's just a little sad. Life goes on and all that."

"But you are happy with Patrice, and you love him?"

"Of course. It is different. That is all. Good. Very good. just not the same."

"And you wouldn't expect it to be."

"No. I have a new marriage and a new life, but losing a spouse... It's unfinished business, and Guillaume will always be a small part of my soul."

She finished the wine and poured another. "It's moments like this that bring it home, that's all."

Geneviève sat back and watched her. "And your trip to Rouen was it fruitful?"

"Yes. Very."

"You've worked it out?"

Pascale nodded. "That James Kerr and Heinrich Vogel were the same man." She said it softly as she sat on the sofa, as though speaking it aloud made it more real. Her chest felt tight. There was a weight to the truth, and now a part of it was revealed, she felt a sense of anticlimax. "Yes. The handwriting on the napkin matched the one on the documents Clarice sent through."

Geneviève smiled. "Inspector Radfield has worked it out as well. The photographs."

Pascale smiled. "Well, different routes, but the same destination, eh?"

"So, now what?"

"Now we still have to find out where *Grand-mère* went." She paused. "I don't suppose you could help?"

Geneviève shook her head. "How many times? It doesn't work like that. I am not omniscient. I just feel things."

"So, not a lot of use, then."

She took the glass out to the kitchen and washed it. By the time she returned to the sitting room, Geneviève had vanished.

"As usual," Pascale said to herself. "Always half a help and half a hindrance." She paused. "But I do miss her when she's gone," she said, her voice a low murmur.

***

As she lay in bed that evening, Patrice by her side, Pascale stared at the shadows stretching across the ceiling, cast by the streetlamp outside. Somewhere, an owl hooted in the distance.

"I spoke to Paul about Guillaume's flat today," she said softly. "Someone's made an offer."

Patrice reached out and took her hand. "How much?"

"One hundred and twenty thousand euros."

"*D'accord*," he said gently. "Less than you hoped. What will you do?"

"I told him to accept. We'll do the paperwork next week."

"Good. It needs to be lived in, and you need to be free."

Silence settled over them again, but he felt her trembling. Quiet, almost imperceptible. He slipped an arm beneath her and drew her close. Her body curled against his, warm, fragile. Her head rested beneath his chin, and he breathed in the faint, familiar scent of her hair.

"I know, *chérie*," he whispered. "I know."

***

Lodève, The Following day.

Clarice was already in the office when Pascale and Patrice arrived. She looked up from her screen and smiled. On the desk was a small replica of the Eiffel Tower, and Pascale chuckled when she saw it.

"Did you have a good trip, madame?"

"Fruitful," Pascale said. "I have a copy of Claire's complete journal. I also brought back some photographs that were missing from the archives in Paris. The little museum at Café Lys Noir is a hidden gem for resistance archives. And I have a letter."

"A letter?"

"Yes, addressed to *Maman*."

"What does it say?"

Pascale shook her head. "I don't know. It has never been opened."

"It's a little family time capsule," Patrice said. He turned to Pascale. "When are you taking it to Colette?"

"As soon as I can. As soon as we clear up the mystery. It's waited long enough."

She went over to the coffee machine, poured two cups, and handed one to Patrice. They both sipped the scalding liquid.

"So, Vanguard was Vogel. Or rather, took his place after the real Vogel presumably met a sticky end in Germany. That answers one mystery," Patrice said. "His behaviour, as described in Claire's journal, starts to make sense in that context."

Clarice looked up from her screen, her mind already racing. "That aligns with the SOE reports I found. Kerr, under the alias Lieutenant Alexander MacGregor, was embedded deep. He had to minimise collateral damage to maintain his cover. A high-ranking SS officer, now that's audacious. What did Claire's journal reveal that we didn't already know?"

Pascale pulled a copied notebook from her bag and placed it on the desk. "She wrote about killing Richter on Vanguard's orders. Aigle and Orage stole a truck and blocked the road. Claire took the shot. But afterwards, there were no reprisals. Vogel—Kerr took over the SS in Rouen, and nothing happened. Claire was suspicious. She mentioned an SS ring and a cigarette case engraved with 'A.K.'"

"But we know he was Vanguard," Clarice said. "So that fits. Still, how did he pull it off? The Gestapo and SS weren't known for being trusting."

"Another puzzle," Pascale said, sipping her coffee. "The deeper we dig, the more complex it all becomes."

Patrice nodded toward the corkboard, where he'd pinned the grainy photograph Radfield had recovered in Berlin—a side-by-side image of Kerr and Vogel, their features eerily similar.

"What we have so far," he said, "is that Kerr killed Vogel in Frankfurt in 1941. Although that's still unconfirmed. Hopefully, David will find something in London. Kerr must have had help to dispose of the body. He then assumed Vogel's identity and operated under deep cover, right under the enemy's noses. Clever. You have to admire the chutzpah. The lack of reprisals after Richter's death was likely calculated. He couldn't risk the SS cracking down and exposing his SOE role."

"So David is still at Kew?" Pascale said.

Clarice pulled a face. "Yes, and *Maman* is not happy about it. She's worried he'll settle back in England and abandon her. She was very irritable last night."

"He dotes on your mother," Pascale said. "There is no chance of his relocating back to England. I'll call her later and smooth things over. She understands the work we do."

"Meanwhile," Patrice said, steering the conversation back on track, "has David found anything useful?"

"He's found SOE records under the alias Alexander MacGregor," Clarice replied. "From late 1941, after his transfer from SIS to SOE, he used that identity. There's nothing under that name in German records, but that's no surprise."

"Has Ingrid uncovered anything about that cultural organisation?" Pascale said.

Clarice shook her head. "No, madame. I spoke with her yesterday, but she's found nothing useful so far. Do you think it might have been a British intelligence front?"

Pascale raised an eyebrow. "Would they have recruited him that young?"

"It does sound far-fetched," Patrice admitted, "but Germany was in chaos. They would have been thinking ahead. Grooming someone for intelligence work, placing him in the SS... it's bold, but not impossible. Worth following up."

"I feel," Pascale said, "that we are picking at scars that never fully healed."

"Hence MI6 getting prickly," Patrice said.

Chapter 12

Lodève, Present Day

The office in Lodève was unusually quiet, a rare moment of solitude for Pascale Hervé. Apart from Clarice interrogating the online world in the outer office, her fingers tapping rhythmically on the keyboard, Pascale had the place to herself. Patrice had taken a day off to spend with Georges and Valérie on a family day together, a welcome break after the intensity of their investigation. Radfield was still in London, digging through the National Archives with Laurence, leaving Pascale with a chance to delve deeper into Claire's journal. She hoped some quiet time with the copied pages might uncover new evidence about her grandmother's fate.

Pascale sat at her desk, the sunshine pouring in through the window from the street outside, casting golden stripes across the worn wooden floor. The sounds of Lodève—distant voices, the hum of a scooter—were muted by the glass, accompanied only by Clarice's occasional typing and the rich aroma of Pascale's coffee. She leafed through the journal, each page pulling her into a world from eighty years ago, a world of shadows and courage she could scarcely imagine.

Then an entry caught her eye, and she started as she read it, a lump rising in her throat. Tears pricked her eyes as the words sank in. "Oh, *Grandpère...*" she whispered, her voice trembling.

"*May 24th, 1944. Radio message from London. Gérard killed in action. Monte Cassino. Devastated. All this for nothing. How do I go on? What is it all for? I hate the Boche. I hate them all.*"

Pascale's fingers hovered over the page, her heart aching for Claire. She had known so little of her grandparents, and her heart ached for the young woman who was a widow before she had a chance to be a wife. She turned a few more pages, and another entry stopped her cold.

"*May 27, 1944. We ambushed a German truck. Aigle and Orage blocked the road. We killed everyone. Driver was young. Married. I saw the ring. Felt sick. Someone will get the same message I got. I hate this war.*"

Pascale closed the journal with a soft thud. She stood, a small tremor passing through her body. She turned to look out the window, the bustling street below a stark contrast to the violence of Claire's world. Then she glanced back toward the outer office, where Clarice was still deep in her work, her youthful focus untouched by the horrors Pascale had just read. Two generations had grown up without having to make the decisions someone of Clarice's age, like Claire, had faced during the war. "May they never do," Pascale said aloud, her voice quiet.

"Did you say something, Madame?" Clarice called from the other room, her tone curious but distracted.

"Nothing, Clarice," Pascale replied, wiping a tear from her cheek. "I was just thinking aloud."

She sat back down, the journal still closed on her desk. Claire's words lingered, a haunting reminder of the cost of resistance and the humanity that persisted even amidst the violence. Pascale knew she had to keep digging, not just for the truth, but for the legacy of a woman who had sacrificed so much.

***

Rouen, May 24th, 1944

Claire Lemoine pedalled her bicycle through the outskirts of Rouen, the late spring air warm against her skin but doing little to ease the tightness in her chest. She was headed for Anton Marchand's cycle shop, an ancient structure of stone and faded timbers that had become a hub of resistance activity under the guise of civilian business. With fuel scarce and cars requisitioned by the Germans, bicycles had become most locals' main mode of transport, and Marchand's emporium was doing a healthy trade.

She stopped outside, leaning her bike against the weathered wall, and entered the main shop. Suzanne Moreau sat at her desk, managing the ledger, but she stood immediately upon seeing Claire. "Claire," she said, her voice warm but tinged with concern. "He's in the workshop."

They went to the back, where Anton Marchand was bent over a bicycle frame, his hands blackened with grease. He looked up as they entered, setting down his tools to greet Claire with a kiss on each cheek, his expression softening. "Good to see you, Claire," he said.

"It's time for London to call," Claire said.

"Of course," Marchand wiped his hands on a rag and led them through the workshop to a narrow staircase at the back. They climbed up to the attic, a cramped space that smelled of dust and oil, where the SOE radio set was hidden beneath a loose floorboard. Marchand assembled the aerial with practised ease, tuning the set to the frequency they'd been given for their scheduled transmission window. He was a skilled operator, having served as a signaller in the French Army during the Great War, and he understood the importance of speed and precision.

Claire watched as he listened through the headphones, the faint beeps and buzzes of Morse code filling the silence. After exactly 30 seconds, the message stopped—short enough to evade German triangulation, they hoped. Marchand sent a brief acknowledgement, a burst of 5 seconds, then began decoding the message, his pencil scratching across the paper in a clear, steady hand.

But as he wrote, his hand froze, and he looked up at Claire, his eyes filled with sorrow. "*Chérie*, I am so sorry," he said, his voice barely above a whisper.

"What is it?" Claire said, snatching the paper from his hand, her eyes scanning the words. The message, in Anton's neat script, hit her like a physical blow: "Message for Flamme. STOP Gérard Lemoine KIA Monte Cassino. STOP Condolences. AS. STOP"

"Noooooo! No! No!" Claire's cry tore through the attic, raw and anguished, as she staggered back. Suzanne reached out, wrapping an arm around her to steady her as tears flooded Claire's eyes, spilling down her cheeks. Her body shook with the aching loss, the weight of Gérard's death crashing over her like a tidal wave. She clutched the paper. Her sobs echoed in the small space as Suzanne held her tight, whispering words of comfort that Claire couldn't hear through her grief. "You knew it was possible. But we never expect it. We never do."

"Oh, Gérard, *mon amour*," she said, sobbing in Suzanne's arms. "I told him not to go. But duty. Duty called."

"As it did for you, *Chérie*," Suzanne said, holding her tight. "As it did for you."

***

Outskirts of Rouen, May 27th, 1944

Three days after the devastating news of Gérard's death, Claire stood on the outskirts of Rouen, her Sten gun slung over her shoulder, her eyes hard with a resolve born of grief and fury. Anton Marchand and André Fournier waited beside a stolen truck, its bonnet propped up to feign a breakdown. Claire and Suzanne crouched behind a low stone wall, their weapons ready, the tension between them palpable but unspoken. A truck loaded with ammunition. For the taking.

The rumble of an approaching vehicle broke the silence. A German supply truck, escorted by a motorcycle and sidecar, came into sight. Marchand played his part, gesturing helplessly at the engine as Fournier hopped into the driver's seat, ready to move. The motorcycle rider stood on the pegs and shouted at them to clear the road, his voice sharp with irritation, but Marchand shrugged, pointing again at the engine compartment. The rider's agitation grew, his hand reaching for his sidearm.

"Now!" Claire hissed.

Suzanne and Claire leapt out from behind the wall, Sten guns raised. Claire pulled the trigger. Click. Nothing.

"*Merde!*"

She remembered Freddie McTaggart's words echoing in her head.

"If the bastard jams, and it will, smack the magazine, make sure it's seated. It may have misaligned a round. Pull back the bolt handle, like so." He pointed to the weapon. *"You can visually check or feel to identify if a round is stuck halfway out of the chamber or jammed at an angle..."*

"In the heat of the moment," Claire said, "we will have time for this?"

McTaggart glowered. *"It's that or the enemy kills you, so you learn to do it fast. Later, we will be putting you under real pressure, but even that won't be like the real thing when the enemy is trying to kill you. Now, do it and do it again."*

Practice, practice, practice until they could do it with muscle memory alone.

"If you have to, eject the magazine. Go on, do it. Then put it back. Again! Now, rack the bolt, come on, Jerry's closing in, you are being pelted by machine gun fire, those lads have Mausers. They won't be jamming like this thing. It's effective when it works, but when it doesn't, it can be bloody unreliable, so you need to fix it quickly. Come on, Mrs Lemoine, you are under fire, move! Move! Move!"

"*Merde! Merde! Merde!*" she said, the sweat trickling into her eyes, despite the cold. A bullet snapped by, kicking up stone dust as she rapped the magazine and pulled back the bolt handle, while Suzanne was returning fire. She lifted the Sten and tried again, it kicked and bucked as it spat out bullets, ripping into the motorcycle rider.

The motorcycle crew fell instantly, their bodies crumpling to the ground under the hail of fire. Claire shifted her aim to the truck's cab, the windscreen shattering as bullets tore through it, the driver and his passenger thrown back in a spray of blood. The gunfire stopped as quickly as it began, the air thick with the smell of cordite and petrol.

Marchand and Fournier moved swiftly to the back of the German truck, pulling out crates of ammunition, medical supplies, and a few rifles—anything useful for the resistance. They transferred the haul to their vehicle, working with the efficiency of men who knew they had minutes before a patrol might arrive.

Claire approached the cab, her boots crunching on the gravel as she checked the bodies. The truck driver's lifeless eyes stared up at her, his youthful face frozen in death. As she opened the door, his hand flopped out, a wedding ring glinting on his finger. For a moment, Claire froze, the sight hitting her in the stomach. Another young man dead. Another widow somewhere, just like her, waiting for news that would shatter her world. Guilt gnawed at her, but she pushed it down, her jaw tightening.

I don't have time for this.

"Everything alright?" Marchand called, his voice cutting through her thoughts as he hefted a crate into their truck.

"*D'accord*," Claire replied, her tone flat, though her heart was anything but steady.

"Well, time we weren't here," Marchand said, pulling a canteen of petrol from the truck. He doused the German vehicle, the acrid smell filling the air, and struck a match. The truck erupted in flames as they piled into their own vehicle, the explosion echoing behind them as they made their escape down the winding road.

Chapter 13

Kew, Present Day

David Radfield settled into the quiet atmosphere of the National Archives reading room, the weight of the previous day's concerns lifting slightly. Free from the shadow of surveillance now that Geoffrey Spencer had confirmed that MI6 and DGSI were no longer watching him, he could focus entirely on the task at hand. The SOE records lay before him, a labyrinth of coded messages, operational logs, and personnel files. Having already established that Lt. Alexander MacGregor, aka Vanguard, was parachuted into Germany in 1941, Radfield now trawled through the archives for any mention of Heinrich Vogel, the SS officer whose identity MacGregor had assumed.

His fingers paused on a yellowed page, a faint thrill of discovery cutting through the monotony. It was a radio message, terse and coded, dated October 1941:

"*Frankfurt Station. STOP. Vanguard arriving this PM. STOP. Assassination of target 'Der Rabe'. STOP. Clean-up 11:45. STOP.*"

A brief acknowledgement followed, scrawled in a different hand: "*Received. Proceed.*"

Radfield leaned back in his chair, exhaling slowly. "So, that's why you flew to Germany rather than France," he said to himself, his mind racing. "*Der Rabe...* the Raven. That's got to be Vogel." He glanced at the surrounding pages, searching for more. "I almost admire the audacity. Anything else, I wonder?"

He was so deep in the archives that he almost didn't hear the soft footsteps behind him. His heart jolted, and he spun around, half-expecting a return visit from Spencer. Instead, he saw Laurence Gunthier, her eyes bright with mischief and affection.

"Laurence!" Radfield said, his voice mixed with surprise and relief. "What are you doing here?"

She leaned forward, her dark hair falling about her face, and kissed him lightly on the cheek, her warmth a welcome contrast to the sterile air of the reading room. "Pascale called," she said, settling into the chair beside him. "She told me the intelligence services aren't watching you anymore, so there was no reason for me not to accompany you. I think I was getting on Clarice's nerves, and she ratted on me to Pascale. Now, where are we?"

Radfield smiled, not even considering an argument, as she wouldn't have listened anyway. "Vanguard landed in Germany and assassinated Vogel, taking his place," he said, bringing her up to speed. He pointed to the radio message. "This confirms it. October 1941, Frankfurt. He killed Vogel and assumed his identity to infiltrate the SS."

Laurence nodded, her expression focused as she pulled a stack of files toward her. For a while, they worked in companionable silence, the rustle of paper and the occasional scratch of a pen the only sounds between them. Then Laurence paused, her finger tracing a line on a document.

"David, what is this?" she asked, her voice tinged with excitement. "It mentions Claire Lemoine."

Radfield leaned over her shoulder, his eyes narrowing as he read the faded typescript. "Ah, now, that is interesting," he said, his voice low with anticipation. "It's an extraction note. What's the date?"

"September 1944," Laurence replied, her brow furrowing as she scanned the details. "It says she was evacuated via the Pyrenees, under orders from SOE. Destination: London. Escort unnamed. No mention of arrest, injuries, or subsequent debrief. Just... gone." She looked up. "Then what?"

Radfield sat back, his mind racing to connect the dots. "So, what happened in 1944 that was so significant?" he mused aloud, his thoughts drifting to the turbulent final months of the war in France.

***

Heinrich Vogel's Office, Rouen, July 1944

Vogel sat at his desk with the early morning papers spread across it. The French ones were primarily crowing about Allied gains in Normandy and Italy. Not that he needed a newspaper to tell him about the Normandy bridgehead. From here, he could hear the artillery fire, and from time to time, aircraft flew over. Italy was lost. France, he felt, wouldn't be so far behind, and then? He sighed. The war was lost; it was but a matter of time. *Here we go again.*

The German papers were more worrying. The attempted assassination of the Führer was splashed across the front pages. He tapped his fingers on the desk. A part of him thought the unthinkable. Perhaps it would have been better had it succeeded. Now, in the aftermath, the high command would be frantically focused on plotters when they should be concentrating on the war effort.

There was a knock at the door.

"Come."

SS-Hauptsturmführer Dieter Voss pushed open the door and stood, snapping a salute.

I do believe they are getting younger by the day, Vogel thought as he looked up at the young officer. "What is it, Herr Hauptsturmführer?"

Voss handed him a folded piece of paper. "Message from Berlin, Herr Obersturmfürher."

Vogel took it and read the contents. He froze, his eyes widening slightly. He looked up at Voss, whose face gave nothing away. He carefully folded the message and put it on the desk. His breathing grew more rapid as the news struck home.

"Berlin, Voss." He looked up. "Of course."

"Yes, Her Obersturmfürher."

"Dismissed."

Voss clicked his heels and snapped a salute. "Heil Hitler."

"Heil Hitler."

Voss went out and shut the door behind him. Vogel picked up the paper again. His cousin, Erich Drexler had been implicated in the plot. "Bloody fool," he said almost to himself. But that wasn't enough; that cast doubt on his loyalty, so he was summoned to Berlin to give an account of himself. For a few moments, he sat, thinking, playing out possibilities. What had Erich said to implicate him? Any man put under enough pressure would say anything, implicate anyone to make it stop. Erich would be no different. Driven by paranoia, High Command would be seeking anyone who might be involved. The ripples had spread out to Rouen. "Yes, he said softly to himself, "better they had succeeded."

Then he made a decision. He stood, put on his coat and hat and walked to the door.

The main office was buzzing with conversation, but it fell silent as he came out of his office. He cast a look around, and no one met his eye except Voss, who maintained steady eye contact.

"I am going out for about an hour," he said.

"Herr, Obersturmfürher?" Grey eyes staring boring through his soul, seeking his hidden demons. Suspicion or curiosity? Or was that just wishful thinking?

Scheiße! He knows.

"I have some unfinished business to take care of." He looked at his watch. "Make the necessary preparations for my journey to Berlin, Herr Hauptsturmführer."

"Very good, Herr, Obersturnmfürher." Again, he snapped a salute. "Heil Hitler."

"Heil Hitler."

Vogel walked out of the building and down the steps, wondering if his coat was too warm for this time of the year, yet his blood didn't feel warm. If he went to Berlin, he would be dead within days, maybe as few as hours. He couldn't take that risk. He had one last chance, one last gamble, one last hand to play. There was one person, the only person, he hoped he could turn to for help.

Eschewing his staff car, he walked briskly with purpose, his breath coming in sharp gasps. He kept a wary eye out for any followers, but he didn't see any and relaxed slightly. He then followed the small roads and alleys to Café Lys Noir.

***

Frankfurt, 1941.

James Kerr had landed on the outskirts of the city the previous night. Having buried his parachute, he walked toward the city in the darkness. He knew exactly where he was going. Dressed in a dark suit and coat with a fedora hat, he moved purposefully to the suburbs, where he came to a housing estate. There, apartment blocks loomed in silent rows. He circled until he found the one he was looking for. Walking up the narrow stairs, he reached the door he was looking for. He smiled at the familiar name on the nameplate. He knocked.

"Coming, just a moment." A voice came from inside.

A moment later, the door opened.

"Heinrich," James said. "It's been a while."

Vogel looked at his visitor with a mixture of recognition and suspicion, his hand lingering on the doorframe. "Yames? What are you doing here? I've not seen you since school." He absently rubbed his jaw where James had landed a right jab all those years ago, his eyes narrowing slightly.

"Aren't you going to invite me in?"

Vogel hesitated, then stepped aside as politeness or curiosity won over. "Yes, come in."

He closed the door behind James and led him to the small front room. "Do you want a drink, Yames?"

"No, thank you, Heinrich."

"Well, what do you want?"

"So it's true, you've joined the SS. Didn't see that coming, Heinrich. I had you down for a commission in the Wehrmacht, given your family history." He paused, hands in pockets as he looked about the room, taking in the tidiness, the almost lack of a lived-in feel. Sparse furniture, no pictures, nothing that resembled personality. It was a place to sleep and little else.

"Yes. I felt this was a better career option, Yames. I joined the party. I presume you did, too?"

"Of course. I am a loyal German."

"I am being deployed to Rouen to sort out the resistance there. Like cockroaches, they are. What are you doing for the cause, Yames?"

James didn't answer directly. "Rouen. Yes, I am headed that way, too."

"Oh, maybe we can travel together."

Had Heinrich Vogel been quicker on the uptake, he might have seen what was coming. It might have saved his life.

"No, I will be travelling alone," James said, moving his hand from his pocket. Vogel was too slow; he missed the knife in James' hand, and it was through his ribs and into his heart before he could react. His eyes widened, and he gave a little cough as he died. James embraced the body as the life expired and lowered it gently to the floor as he had been trained. As the light faded from Vogel's eyes, Kerr felt a flicker of guilt, quickly suppressed. He thought he would feel more. Remorse or regret, just that slight flicker then nothing. That momentarily surprised him. Otto's voice echoed in his mind: "*Alles klar*, James. Ready for what's next."

He went into the bathroom, took out some dark hair dye from a small pouch, and spent the next hour dyeing his hair. He looked in the mirror. The self-inflicted injury from the previous summer on his brow had faded to a neat scar that matched the one on Vogel's brow. The one he had given him all those years ago. His newly darkened hair gave him enough of a resemblance to pass.

He dressed in Vogel's SS uniform and checked himself in the mirror again. It was a good fit, he told himself. Even the boots fitted perfectly without pinching. It sat well, the thought as he studied his reflection. Maybe a little too well.

Before leaving, Kerr slipped Vogel's SS ring from his finger, pocketing it alongside the cigarette case. A trophy to seal the deception.

He went into the front room and sat by the body. He took out his cigarette case and smoked a cigarette while he waited. Eventually, there was a knock at the door. He rose, walked to the door, and opened it. Two men he had never met before and would never meet again stood there, holding a rolled-up carpet. One of them nodded slightly. "The Lysander flies at dawn," he said, his voice low.

"In the front room," Kerr said. He closed the door behind them and watched as they unrolled the carpet, placed Vogel's body in it, and rolled it back up. They hefted the carpet and went back to the door. Kerr let them out and closed the door behind them. He glanced at his watch. "Time I wasn't here; I have a train to catch."

He went into the bedroom, took Vogel's leather coat from the wardrobe, and put it on, adjusting it until it hung correctly. Again, a good fit. Picking up the cap, he made his way to the door, closing it behind him. He put the cap on, adjusting it to a rakish angle, and walked down the steps to the street.

***

Rouen, Late July 1944

The door of Café Lys Noir flew open with a sharp crash, the hinges groaning as Heinrich Vogel—or the man posing as him—strode inside. Behind the counter, Marguerite Fournier looked up from wiping a glass, her breath catching at the sight of the SS officer. His black uniform gleamed with an air of menace, the silver skull on his cap catching the dim light. She opened her mouth to speak, but the words died in her throat as he marched straight toward her, his boots echoing on the wooden floor.

"Where is Flamme?" Vogel demanded, his voice low and urgent, his German accent clipped but laced with an undercurrent of tension.

"Herr Vogel..." Marguerite began, her hands trembling as she set the glass down.

"Don't waste my time," he snapped, his blue eyes piercing as he stared at her, through her. "Get her here. I'll be upstairs waiting. Go on! Hurry!"

Without waiting for a response, he pushed past the counter and climbed the narrow staircase to the private room above, his movements swift and purposeful.

Shaking, Marguerite fumbled for the telephone, swearing to herself as her fingers fumbled at the holes as she dialled Claire Lemoine's safehouse. "Claire," she said as the line connected, her voice agitated. "It's Vogel. He's here, and he wants to speak to you. You need to get..."

Before she could finish, Vogel had stormed back down the stairs, his patience worn thin. He snatched the phone from her hands, ignoring her startled gasp, and pressed it to his ear. "Claire, get here as soon as you can," he said, his tone softer but no less urgent. "You will come to no harm, but it is urgent. No questions. Just come. Now." He hung up without waiting for a reply and returned upstairs, his expression unreadable.

Claire arrived fifteen minutes later, her breath uneven from the hurried journey through Rouen's shadowed streets. "I got here as soon as I could," she said to Marguerite, her voice steady despite the tension in the air.

"Is he upstairs?" Marguerite's face was deathly white, her eyes darting toward the staircase. She gestured to the upstairs room and nodded, unable to speak. Claire said nothing more, her jaw tightening as she climbed the steps to the room where she had so often met Vanguard.

She pushed open the door and stood in the threshold, her gaze locking onto the man inside. The room was normally lit, and for the first time, the light fell harshly on the man she knew as Vanguard, stripping away the shadows in which he had once hidden. No longer was he pretending, and there was a palpable tension in his posture. His shoulders squared, hands clasped tightly behind his back, but there was a slight tremble, and as he turned, she could see the patina of sweat on his brow. The SS uniform still clung to him, but his face held something else. She stopped as she recognised it. *Fear.*

My God, the man is afraid..

"Vanguard?" she said, her voice low, testing the suspicion that had been growing in her mind for months.

He nodded, a faint, almost resigned smile tugging at his lips.

"I thought as much a while ago," Claire said, stepping into the room and closing the door behind her. "You left clues. Your ring, the '*Alles Klar*' on the cigarette case, and the lack of reprisals after Richter's death. Why did you want him dead? I have to ask."

Vogel—or Vanguard—sighed, his shoulders slumping slightly. "He was going to Berlin," he said simply. "He would have discovered the truth." He shrugged, as if the murder of an SS officer were a mere inconvenience.

"And now?" Claire pressed, her eyes narrowing as she studied him.

"Earlier this month, they tried to assassinate the Führer," he said, his voice dropping to a near whisper. "You've heard, I'm sure."

"Yes," Claire replied, her tone bitter. "A pity they failed."

"I've been recalled to Berlin," he continued, ignoring her jab. "Somehow, I have been implicated in the plot."

"How?"

"Vogel's cousin implicated Heinrich. They are spreading the net wide now. There is panic at the top. Anyone can be implicated. Guilt or innocence is of no matter. I cannot go to Berlin. If I do, I'm done for. If they don't hang me as Vogel, they'll execute me as a spy."

Claire crossed her arms, her mind racing. "What do you want me to do?"

She took a slow breath, her eyes not leaving his. He had been her link to London, her handler in the dark, during those meetings here in this room with his face hidden, disguising his voice. But that uniform... and the blood on his hands...

"Get me to Spain," he said, his voice steady but laced with desperation.

Her eyes widened, and a mix of incredulity and anger flashed across her face. "What? You cannot be serious. You're the Boche. I cannot ask operatives to move a high-ranking SS officer. The risk is too great."

"I am more than able to disguise myself, Claire," he said, stepping closer, his tone earnest. "I've been doing it all my life. Today, I am Heinrich Vogel, but tomorrow, I can take the place of an Allied airman. No one will know. I speak English like a native, because I am a native."

Claire stared at him, her heart pounding as she weighed the risks. Vanguard had been her handler, her ally in the shadows, but he was also the enemy, or at least he had been playing the part. Could she trust him now? Had she ever truly known him at all?

***

Café Lys Noir, Rouen, July 1944

Claire Lemoine sat at the head of the table in the upstairs room of Café Lys Noir, her posture rigid but composed, but her tension was betrayed by the tapping of her fingers on the table. Around her, a storm of emotions was brewing among her resistance cell. Around the table sat Jean-Luc Dufresne, Anton Marchand, Suzanne and the Fourniers—André and Marguerite—each face etched with a mix of suspicion, anger, and uncertainty. The air was thick with the weight of Vanguard's revelation: the man they'd known as Obersturmführer Heinrich Vogel, a high-ranking SS officer, was in fact James Kerr, a British SOE agent who had been their handler all along.

"Where is the bastard now?" Marchand demanded, his voice rough with barely contained fury, his hands clenched into fists on the table. "I'll happily kill him now and save us all trouble."

"In the safe house at Malaunay," Claire replied, her tone steady despite the fire in her own chest. She understood their anger—she felt it too—but now was not the time for emotion to cloud their judgment.

"And how do we know it isn't compromised?" Marchand said, his eyes narrowing.

"Because, if it is, he was the one who compromised it," Claire said, shaking her head. "I know, this is as much a shock to me as it is to you, but the man we've known as Obersturmführer Vogel has been our SOE contact all along."

"But he was there, taking part in the reprisals," Marchand said, his face twisted with rage, the memory of executed civilians flashing in his eyes. Claire met his gaze but kept her face calm. The anger burned inside her, too, but she forced it down. She had to lead.

"Look, I understand," she said, her voice firm but empathetic. "But this man is a risk to us if he goes to Berlin. If he stays here, the Gestapo will pick him up and take him anyway. His game is up. His cover is blown."

"How can we trust him?" Marguerite said, her voice quieter but no less intense. Until now, she had remained silent, letting the men grill Claire, but her question cut through the room like a knife. "Well?"

Claire sighed, the weight of the interrogation pressed on her shoulders just as she had pressed Vanguard earlier. "We don't," she said. "Maybe we never could, knowing what we now know."

"A British agent taking part in brutal reprisals," Jean-Luc muttered, his tone laced with disgust.

"A British agent who fed us vital information because he was embedded in the SS," Claire countered, her voice sharp. "Remember that. He gave us targets, warned us of raids. Saved lives, even if his hands aren't clean."

"After that disaster at Malaunay, that wasn't always the best, was it?" Marchand said. And what about La Silhouettes? All hanged. What about that, eh? The bastard was there."

Claire shrugged, conceding the point with a slight tilt of her head. It cost her nothing to acknowledge their failures, but it didn't change the reality they faced. "I know, I know. The truth is," she said, her voice steady, "we have no option."

"We do," André Fournier said, his voice low and dangerous. He slipped his hand into his pocket and placed his Webley pistol on the table slowly, deliberately, as if offering a vote that spoke louder than words in the silent room, the metal glinting in the dim light. "He's a liability. British agent or not. We finish it here. One life for the sake of the many."

Claire's eyes flicked to the pistol, then up to meet André's gaze. She saw the resolve in his expression, the same thought that had crossed her mind when Vanguard first revealed himself. But she shook her head, her decision unshakable. "No," she said. "We get him out. Unless I get authorisation from London to do otherwise. As it is, London wants him extracted, so we follow our orders. We extract him as if he were any other Allied asset. That's the plan, and that's what we do. Anton, André, Jean-Luc, you're with me. We take him south. Marguerite and Suzanne, you'll remain here. Am I clear?"

"But..." Marchand began, his voice rising in protest.

"No buts," Claire cut him off, her tone brooking no argument. "That's the plan. We stick to it. We're moving him tonight. D'accord?"

She looked around the room, meeting their eyes one by one, her gaze steady and unyielding. There was no dissent, just a quiet 'd'accord' from each of them, though the tension in their expressions remained. Claire nodded, satisfied. "Let's get to it, then."

As the group rose to prepare for the night's operation, Claire lingered momentarily, her hand resting on the back of her chair. The weight of her decision settled on her shoulders, heavy but necessary. Vanguard—Kerr—might be an ally, but he was also a liability, and the journey to Spain would test them all.

Chapter 14

Berlin, Present Day

Ingrid Keller's office at the Bundesarchiv in Berlin was a calm sanctuary heavy with the weight of history. Her desk was piled high with files and her computer screen was glowing with digitised records. Since Radfield's visit, she had been busy with other work, her role as an archivist demanding her attention. But when a quiet moment finally presented itself, her curiosity drew her back to David Radfield's research request. The trail had been cold at first. The records regarding the Kulturverein für Heimkehr, a supposed cultural organisation for German repatriation in the 1920s, were frustratingly vague, filled with bureaucratic dead ends. Whichever trail she followed, she came up against the same dead ends. She was, however, nothing if not tenacious.

"There has to be something."

Her breakthrough came when she stumbled upon a reference to Otto Reinhardt in a cross-referenced personnel file from the Weimar era. Deciding to change tack, she pulled every record she could find on Reinhardt, her interest piqued by the name tied to the organisation Radfield had flagged.

"Oh my, Otto, you had quite the career," she said to herself, leafing through the brittle documents with a historian's reverence.

Born in 1850, Otto Reinhardt had served in the Prussian Army during the Franco-Prussian War of 1870–1871, fighting in the pivotal Battle of Sedan. "Mm, you were awarded the Iron Cross Second Class for that," Ingrid murmured, a smile playing on her lips as she read the citation for bravery leading a charge in the face of enemy fire. "You were a brave man, Otto. And I think I like you."

She paused at an old photograph, the sepia tone capturing a stiff young man in a pickelhaube with a military moustache that curled upwards at the ends, his eyes staring back from over a century ago. There was a quiet dignity in his gaze, a love for Germany that seemed to radiate through the faded image. Ingrid felt an unexpected connection to this man she'd never met, a distinguished young officer whose life had been shaped by war and duty. There was, she thought, something admirable about this man. As so often happened, she wished she could meet the subjects of her research, and Otto was no exception. "The tales you could tell, Otto," she said quietly, looking at the picture. "If only I could ask."

She continued leafing through the file. "Ah, injured and repatriated. Medical discharge. But that didn't stop you, did it?"

Further records detailed Reinhardt's return to service at the outbreak of the Great War in 1914. "A staff officer," she said to herself, her interest piqued. "Then transferred. That's interesting. Transferred to Abteilung IIIb. Now, that is *very* interesting. Very interesting indeed."

Abteilung IIIb was the Prussian General Staff's intelligence branch during WWI, responsible for espionage and codebreaking. This was a fitting role for a seasoned officer like Reinhardt, who was too old for the front but invaluable back in Berlin. "What did you do after that, Otto, you old rogue?"

The records traced Reinhardt's career through the turmoil of the post-war years, following the Treaty of Versailles. Then, a detail caught her eye: the Kulturverein für Heimkehr. Formed in 1920, the organisation listed Reinhardt as an employee. "So I come full circle."

She tapped her teeth with her pencil as she pondered the significance of the find. "Only two years before you went to Scotland to bring James Kerr over," Ingrid said, her mind racing. "What's the significance?" She sat back and chewed on her pencil. "I am back where I started, Otto Reinhardt and the Kulturverein für Heimkehr. There's something I'm missing here, but what is it?"

She returned to the Kulturverein für Heimkehr records, this time trying a different tactic: "Follow the money, Ingrid, follow the money."

Digging into financial ledgers and correspondence, she finally found what she sought. Discreet payments funnelled through the organisation, coded in a way that screamed intelligence work. "There's skulduggery here and you were at the heart of it, weren't you, Otto, you old rogue. You thought I wouldn't find out, didn't you?"

The Kulturverein für Heimkehr wasn't a cultural group at all. It was a front for the Abwehr, the Weimar Republic's nascent intelligence service, established to circumvent the Versailles restrictions.

"Oh, you crafty old devil," Ingrid said with a smile and admiration for the man who had played such a long game. This wasn't just intelligence work; this was recruiting for the long game. They planned Kerr's recruitment from the beginning. She picked up the telephone and dialled, barely able to contain her excitement and eager to share her discovery.

"Clarice Gunthier?" she asked when the line connected.

"Yes, speaking," Clarice said.

"Ingrid Keller. Your English gentleman asked me to call you if I found anything about the Kulturverein für Heimkehr."

"And you have," Clarice said, and Ingrid could almost hear the smile on the other end.

"Oh yes, Madame, I have. The Kulturverein für Heimkehr was an Abwehr front. Does that help your investigation?"

There was a brief silence, then Clarice's voice returned, tinged with awe. "Oh, my, yes. I need to tell the others. Thank you so much, Fräulein."

"You're welcome," Ingrid said warmly. "It was a fascinating journey."

She hung up with a satisfied smile, unaware that every word of their conversation had been intercepted and monitored by an MI6 team that had tapped Clarice's line weeks ago as part of their surveillance of Pascale Hervé's investigation.

85 *Albert Embankment, London, Present Day*

Maggie Blunt strode into Geoffrey Spencer's office at MI6 headquarters, her usual composure replaced by a sense of urgency. The door swung shut behind her. The view of the Thames through the tinted windows of the room cast a gentle grey light, and Spencer looked up, disturbed by her unusually dramatic entrance.

"Don't you knock these days, Maggie?" Spencer asked, looking up from his desk with a raised eyebrow, though his tone held a trace of amusement.

"Sorry, sir. You need to listen to this," Maggie handed him a tablet with the intercepted audio queued up.

She sat as Spencer listened to the recording of Ingrid Keller's call to Clarice Gunthier. As he heard the words 'Abwehr front,' he looked up, his expression darkened, and his jaw tightened.

"They really should stop using landlines," she said when it had finished.

"Bugger," Spencer said. "I had hoped they wouldn't get this far." He sighed. "Even got the Germans working for them. That Radfield is a canny investigator. Got to give them that."

"Now what?" Maggie asked, her arms crossed, waiting for direction. "Are you going to tell me what is going on?"

He narrowed his eyes. "I suppose you know enough now to tell you. So he did.

"Oh," she said when he had finished.

"Oh indeed." Spencer leaned back in his chair, his mind racing. The Abwehr connection tied James Kerr, aka Vanguard, directly to German intelligence as early as 1922, confirming suspicions that his role as a double agent was far deeper than MI6 records suggested. Now, Pascale's team were about to uncover secrets MI6 had buried for decades. Secrets that could make the Philby affair look like a minor indiscretion. "Bugger."

"So you said. What are we going to do about it?"

"I need a flight to Béziers as soon as possible," Spencer said, his voice firm. "And I want all of those people in Lodève."

"Keller as well?" Maggie said, her brow furrowing.

"All of them," Spencer confirmed, his tone leaving no room for argument. "Every single one. And the investigating police officer, what's his name?"

"Capitaine François Viala."

"Yes, that's the chap. Him too. Arrange travel for Keller and make it clear she has no option. Speak to the people in Berlin if you have to. Twist arms if you must."

"And then?" Maggie pressed, sensing there was more to his plan.

"And then, I play my ace," Spencer said, grim determination etched on his face. "It's all I have. It will either bury this thing or blow it wide open, but I have no choice."

Maggie nodded, already pulling out her phone to arrange the logistics, while Spencer turned to the window, his gaze fixed on the Thames. The truth about Vanguard was a Pandora's box, one he'd hoped would stay closed. But with Pascale Hervé and her team closing in, he had no choice but to act, and hope his contingency plan would be enough to contain the fallout.

***

Lodève

Pascale picked up her telephone. "Monsieur Caron, what have you got?"

"Good day, Madame. I have some information. We have been searching the area around the remains we found at the bottom of the gully. There wasn't much, but we found some artefacts."

"Anything of interest?"

"Two things. A signet ring with the SS emblem on it and, er, an antique cigarette case. It's very old, late nineteenth or early twentieth century. It has initials engraved on it. Does 'A.K.' mean anything to you?"

Pascale chuckled. "It means, doctor, I can identify your body."

France, 1944

Suzanne came to the Café Lys Noir the evening before their departure, clutching a satchel containing the forged papers. Claire sat at a corner table, clouded in cigarette smoke and the smell of cognac. The room was quiet at this time of the evening, as Marguerite was about to close. A few people still lingered, and the only sound apart from low voices was the clinking of glasses as Marguerite busied herself cleaning them while looking across at Claire and Suzanne.

At his usual table, Klaus Falkenrath sat taking his time over a brandy.

Marguerite nodded to Claire, who came up to the bar. Marguerite nodded towards Falkenrath. "He won't go. Keeps drinking brandy. We need to get rid of him."

Claire nodded. "Get André. I think the time has come for Herr Falkenrath."

Marguriete narrowed her eyes, but said nothing, going out to the back to fetch André.

Claire walked across to Falkenrath's table, clutching a fresh glass of brandy. She sat opposite him and pushed the glass across. Falkenrath stared at her through inebriated eyes. "Frau... I don't know your name..."

"No. We've never been introduced properly, Herr Falkenrath. You can call me Claire."

Falkenrath reached out a hand, and she took it.

"Pleased to meet you, Claire." He gulped the brandy.

"I've been watching you."

She sat, perfectly still, ignoring the icy chill in her spine.

"Have you?"

"I know what goes on here."

"And what is that?"

"Upstairs. I see you and various men." He looked across at Suzanne. "Her, too." He paused, the thoughts collecting in his disoriented mind. "A place like this? Better left to its... pleasures..."

Claire smiled inwardly. *He's picked up the melody but missed the tune here.*

"The war is lost," he was saying, his mind drifting with the alcohol.

"I know. The Reich is finished. It is only a matter of time, Herr Falkenrath."

"Call me Klaus. I cannot stay here. I must go back to the Fatherland, you know this? If I had more time, I would have shut this place down."

"Yes, of course. You are a loyal servant of the Reich."

"I am, Frau Claire. I am."

"Would you like to go upstairs, Herr Falkenrath?"

He looked at her, his eyes barely focusing. She smiled, showing her even white teeth. She reached out a hand and touched his gently, ignoring the feeling of revulsion. "Come on. Just you and I, Kalus."

"Why not?" he said, trying to rise unsteadily to his feet. She moved round quickly, catching him as he swayed. Hooking an arm under his, she supported him as she walked him behind the bar and to the back of the building, to the stairs. Slowly, stumbling one step at a time, they made their way to the upstairs room. Unbeknown to Falkenrath, André followed like a giant cat stalking its prey.

Once in the room, Kauas straightened up slightly and looked around. "This isn't... What I thought..." He stopped suddenly as the cord André slipped over his neck, bit into his trachea, and choked off any sound. He kicked and struggled, his heels drumming on the wooden floor, as he fought for breath, but André was too strong for him. In a couple of minutes, he was lying lifeless on the floor.

"I'll dispose of the body later," André said. "We have other things to deal with right now."

They went back downstairs where the others were all gathered.

***

The whole group were now waiting in the main café where Marguerite had locked the doors and turned the open/closed sign to closed. Claire looked around at them all, still slightly breathless from the murder upstairs.

Suzanne's husband, Pierre, was several years her senior and had spent time in Maison d'Arrêt de Rouen for five years before the war for forgery. Upon coming out, he swore he would go straight. He met Suzanne, and they settled into married life. He took a job as a postman. He once looked at his young wife with her dark, silky hair and bright blue eyes and told her that she made an old man very happy.

The onset of war changed everything. While he maintained his role as a postman, his previous skills as a forger became useful. Instead of forging banknotes, he now spent time preparing identity documents, travel passes, and tickets to aid allied airmen on their journey to Spain. Suzanne went from disapproval of his erstwhile criminal career to encouraging it. That evening, she collected Vanguard's new identity documents and rail passes for the other four and took them to Café Lys Noir.

Usually, they limited the couriers who travelled with the escapees to two to minimise risk to the cell, but this was different, and Suzanne worried. Vogel had a reputation. He was vulnerable now and on the run from the Nazis, but it occurred to her that he was now even more dangerous.

Suzanne slid the satchel to Claire. "They will be on the lookout for him. There are patrols everywhere. They know he is on the run."

Claire sighed, her fingers tracing her journal. "I can't help wondering if André was right. Eliminate the risk."

Suzanne hesitated. Claire always seemed so in control, but now, there was a risk they had never faced before. "Can we trust him?"

Claire shook her head. "I wish I knew, Suzanne. I've had these qualms for a while. Even as far back as Malaunay. That was bad intelligence. Then Richter's assassination and the lack of reprisals. I didn't like the smell of that. I don't know. I wonder whether he has become the man he was impersonating; he's spent so long in the role. 'alles klar,' he says that a lot." She paused. "Last night, I was sorting out everything. Taking his old clothes to burn them. I found something. It might be nothing." She shook her head. "But he is an SOE asset, so we do what London wants."

"What did you find?"

"An old letter from before the war. It was in German from someone he knew."

"We need to speak to London."

Claire nodded. "Ask Anton to contact them. Let them know what is happening. No, on second thoughts." She grabbed a piece of paper and scribbled a note, giving it to Suzanne. "Ask him to send this. We'll check in with them when we get to the safe house at Pau."

Suzanne looked at the message—*Suspect Vanguard's loyalty. Who is Otto Rienhardt? What is Kulturverein für Heimkehr? Request confirmation. Will check at Pau safe house.*

Suzanne took it and read it, raising an eyebrow. "Are you sure?"

Claire shook her head. "No, that's why this message. I'll know for certain when I get their response."

Meanwhile, Marchand and Fournier went back upstairs and brought down Falkenrath's body.

"Check it's clear, Fournier said.

Marguerite went to the door, unlocked it and looked out.

"No one about."

"Good." Marchand and Fournier picked Falkenrath up and went outside. They walked the few hundred meters through the narrow streets, holding the body upright between them as if helping a drunken friend home. The streets were deserted, which suited their scheme. They came to the bank of the Seine. Looking around to see if they were unnoticed, they tipped Falkenrath into the river and melted away into the night.

Back at the café, Claire watched as Suzanne set out, clutching the message for London. She closed the door and looked across at Marguerite. She sighed. She could only hope that London would respond to her request before they reached the Pyrenees. The word that might change everything.

***

Rouen, 1944.

They boarded the train at Gare de Rouen-Rive-Droite to Paris Gare Saint-Lazare. via the Paris–Le Havre line. Claire led them to the third-class carriage, full of weary travellers, the air thick with the smell of old cigarette smoke and sweat. They would blend in more easily in a crowded carriage. The passage through the checkpoint had gone without a hitch, and she could relax a little more now.

Vanguard was dressed in a drab coat and a tatty, wide-brimmed hat that he used to shield his eyes. Claire and the others dressed in rough, worn clothing as French peasants. They sat in the carriage, putting Vanguard in a window seat as far from view of the aisle as possible.

Suzanne stayed behind. She squeezed Claire's hand before they boarded the train. Claire raised an eyebrow in question, and Suzanne gave a brief nod. It was done. Now, there was nothing to do but wait for London's response when they arrived in Pau.

Claire sat opposite Jean-Luc, noting his tension. His fingers fidgeted with his bag, avoiding her gaze. They were all stressed, but he had taken plenty of allied escapees on this route like her. She frowned, and he shook his head. He leaned close and whispered. "I need to talk to you."

"Not here."

He looked around and nodded. He got up and walked back to the corridor. A German soldier passed, his boots clicking on the floor, oddly loud over the sound of the train wheels on the tracks beneath, he glanced disinterestedly at her before continuing, and Claire waited a beat before following.

Once in the noisy connection between coaches, they could speak without being overheard.

"What is it?" she said.

"There's something I need to tell you." He hesitated, looking around. It occurred to her that he was terrified, not just nervous.

"What?" she said. "Spit it out."

He gulped. "It was me. I'm sorry."

"What was?"

"Vogel. He said he would keep my wife from deportation to Germany. I've not seen her since the invasion. He said... If I cooperated..."

"*Merde*! Are you telling me that..." She thought back. The long absences. The time he went missing after the rail sabotage. Things the SS seemed to know. And he was the common link between La Libération and La Silhouettes. It made sense, but deep down, she had avoided confronting those oddities for fear of the truth. "You were betraying us?"

He nodded.

"I should kill you now, you treacherous shit!"

"I am so sorry. But, but, he never seemed to act. He knew about the safe house at Malaunay, which was why I was late. I expected to find you all arrested, but he never did. Now we know why."

"It was pure luck that he was a British agent. *Merde*! *Merde*! *Merde*! You bloody fool. Everything we did was at risk because of you. However, can we trust you again?"

Jean-Luc looked away. He couldn't meet her eyes. "What will you do?"

"Carry on. Vanguard didn't betray us to the SS, so you got away with it."

"That's why he wanted Richter dead. Richter knew about me and was pushing for results. Vogel couldn't let things go on any further. The story about Richter being recalled was nonsense. Richter would never have known he was a plant, but he was getting suspicious about the lack of arrests."

She nodded. "Go back to your seat. For the moment, this conversation never happened and say nothing to the others, got it?"

He nodded and slunk back to his seat, staring down at the floor as he sat, his shoulders slumped. Clare realised that she was staring at a broken man and part of her felt sorry, despite the seething rage.

They alighted at Gare Saint-Lazare. The platform was thick with the odour of steam, the hiss of the locomotives and the sharp barked orders in guttural German voices. The August evening hung heavy, a faint drizzle slicking the cobblestones. Once through the ticket checks, again, without incident, and Claire mentally thanked the skills of Pierre Moreau.

Claire led them south along Rue Saint-Lazare, her shawl pulled tightly around her shoulders, her head down. In his drab coat and tatty wide-brimmed hat, Vanguard kept his head low. Jean-Luc's hands shook as he clutched his bag, avoiding her gaze, while André shadowed Vanguard, with Marchand close behind.

At Place de la Madeleine, they were stopped at a checkpoint. Wehrmacht sentries stood under a swastika banner, Karabiner 98k rifles slung over their shoulders. Claire handed over their forged papers, her pulse steady despite the scrutiny. She glanced at Vanguard, whose fingers gripped his coat pocket, eyes darting to a passing SS officer. He was nervous. Something she'd never seen in him before. The sentry returned their papers and waved them through

"*Guten Abend.*"

Claire exhaled, but Vanguard's unease lingered in her mind.

They followed Boulevard des Capucines to the Opéra Garnier. Its golden facade seemed incongruous with the city's gloom. Along Rue des Pyramides, they reached the Louvre, where another checkpoint awaited them. The sentry's cold stare swept over them, the rustle of papers loud as he rifled through them, looking at the faces, comparing them with the photographs in his hand. To avoid suspicion, they spread out, passing one at a time. Claire went first, her heart pounding as she waited beyond the barrier. Jean-Luc fumbled his papers, earning a sharp look from the sentry, and Claire's jaw tightened. *Not now, Jean-Luc.* His betrayal was still raw, and she hadn't decided what to do about it. Vanguard followed, his face composed but pale. The sentry studied his photograph, then nodded, apparently satisfied. Vanguard walked through, joining Claire.

"Keep going," she said, her voice low, eyes tracking him. She watched him cross the Seine at Pont Neuf, André trailing close, hand in his pocket, ready to grasp the knife he always kept handy. Claire followed along the Left Bank, the Quai d'Austerlitz's damp air was chill despite the sun being well up.

They reunited at Gare d'Austerlitz. They passed through ticket checks and reached the platform, where the night train to Bordeaux waited, its engine hissing. Claire checked her watch, dreading the safe house and what London's response might reveal. The cell stood silent, each face taut, the weight of the journey south pressing down.

***

They dozed through the night, the train rocking a lullaby in the blacked-out carriage. The air hung heavy and stale with sweat and tobacco smoke. Claire spent much of the night watching her companions as they drifted in and out of sleep, her mind in turmoil. André sat stiffly beside Jean-Luc, unaware of his betrayal. Vanguard appeared to sleep with his hat tilted low over his face.

Her mind was in turmoil as thoughts came and went. Flashbacks that were beginning to make sense: The bad intel at Malaunay. Richter's assassination. The initials on the cigarette case. His unease at the checkpoints in Paris. A man embedded too deep, perhaps. Was this man an asset or a threat? she wondered. Had he spent so long under cover in an assumed identity, the identity had assumed him. Was he now Vogel after all?

At some point during the night, she drowsed and woke with a start as the train decelerated, hissing and squealing into Bordeaux. Bleary-eyed, the travellers disembarked onto the station, basking in the warmth of the early morning sun. Again, they had the ritual of the ticket checks, the Wehrmacht soldier appeared bored and disinterested, barely looking at their papers, and again, they went through without comment. Claire walked to the ticket office and asked about the connection to Pau.

"We have just under an hour to wait," she said. They found a bench and waited. Eventually, their train arrived, and as before, they made their way to the third-class carriage and settled down for the two-and-a-half-hour journey.

By early afternoon, they were in Pau. There was a heavy German presence, including Wehrmacht soldiers and some SS. She saw a Gestapo operative further down. She tried not to look and draw attention as they walked towards the exit. Gaston Urrutia, a rail worker who kept the Pau safe house, met them at the station entrance and let them through the town streets.

"Quickly now. The Gestapo are everywhere around here. It's got worse since the landings in Normandy."

They followed him through the narrow streets, which were largely deserted. People stayed in their homes, shutters shut.

Once at the house, Claire briefed the group. "We rest here until tomorrow morning," she said. "We start early. A *passeur* will be here first thing to guide us through the mountains. Any questions?"

"I have one, Vanguard said."

"Go on."

"How far into Spain will you four be accompanying me?"

"We get you to Jaca. From there, you are on your own."

"Very good." He flicked open his cigarette case and took out a cigarette, lighting it before snapping the case shut and secreting it back in his pocket. Claire caught again the engraved initials. A.K. Every time she saw it, it unsettled her, and it did now.

"Now, I suggest you all get some rest." She nodded to Marchand. "Upstairs, Anton."

He nodded and followed. They went into the attic, where he retrieved the radio set and prepared it for transmission. He sent a short five-second burst to London advising readiness to receive. A few moments later, the message came back in a series of dots and dashes. Anton Marchand scribbled the coded message down. Twenty seconds later, the transmission stopped. Anton started transcribing the message with his code book, but stopped after two words. He looked up at Claire. She peered over his shoulder at the two words in his neat hand: "Flamme. Eyes only."

He scraped the chair back and stood. He passed the code book across the table. "I'll leave you to it."

Claire sat at the table and worked through the rest of the message. Then she sat back and sighed, letting the pencil drop.

"*Merde*!" She stared at it briefly before folding the paper carefully and slipping it into her bag. Her hands were steady, but her pulse was not.

***

It was still dark when Claire shook them awake. "Come on, get up. I've got some bread and cheese for the journey and canteens of water. We will be on the trails for a few days, so let's get going."

Before they left, Claire gave her journal to Gaston. He raised his eyebrows. "Madame?"

"Send it to the Café Lys Noir in Rouen," she said.

"But, madame..."

She shook her head. "I might not return. It's all in here for someone, one day."

He nodded. "If you wish, madame."

"*Merci.*"

There was a knock at the door, and Gaston went to answer it. They heard low voices, then Gaston came in, followed by a middle-aged man with a dark, wiry face and lithe frame from spending a lifetime outdoors, dressed in dark clothing and wearing a black beret. He held out a hand. "Koldo Etxebarria," he said.

Claire took his hand and then turned to the group. "Koldo is the *passeur*. He will be guiding us. You will do exactly as he says. Understood?"

There were murmurs and nods of agreement.

"Good. Let's get going."

***

They walked through the early morning mist that hung in the valleys below the mountains, masking the peaks. Koldo led them via the small tracks and trails known only to the Basques who lived there. As they climbed, the going became heavier along with their breathing, and as the sun rose, the air warmed steadily, causing them to perspire. Yet Vanguard seemed untroubled. He strode briskly, shrugging off any discomfort, drinking his water sparingly. When midday came, Koldo signalled for them to stop.

"We rest here," he said. "We will wait until nightfall. We will be passing near farms, and there are collaborators and *milice*. In these parts. You can never tell who is watching and who will report you." He spat and wiped his mouth with the back of his hand.

They found shelter among the trees and rested, eating their bread and cheese and drinking their water. Nearby was a small stream, so they took the opportunity to refill their canteens.

They were on the move again at dusk, skirting farms, startling at the occasional dog bark. There were no people, no farmers who might have given them away, no *milice* patrols, just the sound of footsteps and breathing, occasionally broken up by the sound of an owl. Bats fluttered in the half-light, swooping for prey. Otherwise, they moved steadily without incident.

By the second night, they were in Oloron Saint Marie. They spent the day resting before moving again. The group was weary by now from the forced march, and even Vanguard was showing signs of tiredness. Claire concentrated on the march, allowing her thoughts to wander. She had her plans, but she had not yet decided when she was going to implement them.

From Oloron, they entered the Aspe Valley. Here, the terrain grew steeper, with pine forests and rocky paths. After several days on the trail, constantly walking over rough ground, they were suffering from exhaustion and blisters. They stopped briefly to put plasters on their feet, but Claire drove them on. "Keep moving," she said. "Come on. We cannot stop for too long." They followed shepherd trails parallel to the Gave d'Aspe, climbing steadily toward the Hautes-Pyrénées, eventually arriving at Etsaut, a small village high in the mountains. After five days of steady hiking, this was their final stop before the border.

"We hide in a barn for the day," Koldo said. "When we set out from here, we need to be careful, the Boche *Gebirgsjäger* operate in this area." Again, he expressed his contempt by spitting forcefully and wiping his hand across his mouth.

After a day's rest, they set out again.

***

Col Du Somport, 1944

The path rose sharply, and they worked their way steadily until they reached the entrance to the pass. Koldo stopped and pointed along the narrow, rocky path, barely visible in the dark. "That way, madame, messieurs, is Spain."

"Thank God for that," Jean-Luc said, sitting down and hanging his head on his knees. As they progressed, Claire became increasingly worried about his stamina. He had guided escapees this way before, but something had broken. The confession had finished the man. He had lost the will to carry on, and a part of her felt sorry. She looked at him now more with pity than contempt.

"We keep going, Jean-Luc," she said. "No one is left behind."

Further they went, pausing briefly at any sound, only to realise it was some animal or bird. Eventually, partway through, they came to a cave. "In there," Koldo said. "We rest here for the day."

"They settled down, and as dawn broke, Claire went out onto the path, gesturing to Koldo.

"Koldo, come with me," she said.

He came out and joined here. "What is it, madame?"

"How close are we to the border?"

He shrugged. "Two, maybe three kilometres."

"Show me."

He frowned.

"Show me."

He shrugged and led the way. After about half an hour, the pass widened slightly and started to descend. This, madame, is the border. There," he pointed down the valley, "is Jaca."

Claire started and looked back. "Did you hear that? It sounded like gunfire."

"It was," Koldo said, "and it was too close to our location for my liking."

"Three shots. We need to go back now." Claire pulled her pistol out and walked back the way they had come, moving as quickly as she could on the uneven terrain, looking around for any sign of *Gebirgsjägers* who might have heard the shots and come to investigate. When they arrived back at the cave, Vanguard was waiting outside. Something about his demeanour caused Claire's hackles to rise.

"What are you doing outside?"

"What were you doing?" he said. "We are supposed to be lying low."

"Scouting the final few kilometres," she said. He stood there, saying nothing as she pushed past him and stopped.

"*Merde!* What happened here?"

The cave floor was littered with the bodies of their companions. Fournier and Marchand were sprawled on their backs, eyes staring sightlessly. Marchand and Fournier had dark stains on their chests. Jean-Luc lay face down with a sticky black hole in the back of his skull. *An execution.* She turned slowly and looked at Vanguard, her face twisted in rage, her throat catching with bile.

"You killed them. You killed them all."

"I'm sorry, Claire. But Jean-Luc was a traitor. He had been feeding the SS information. He killed the other two..."

Claire looked down and saw the pistol lying next to Jean-Luc's hand.

"And?"

"I had no choice," he said. "I killed him in self-defence."

"Claire crouched down by the bodies, never quite taking her eye off Vanguard, but he did not attempt to do anything. He just stood there, watching. Guarded, but motionless. Koldo stood next to him, and she could see the tension in his body, but he, too, kept his peace, waiting for her to make a decision.

"We go," she said, standing up and brushing her hands on her clothing. "Now."

"But, it's daylight," Koldo said. "The *Gebirgsjäger*..."

"We take the risk. Come on."

They went outside. "What about the bodies?" Koldo said, crossing himself.

"We leave them where they are, " she said, looking around. There is nowhere to bury them, and we don't have the time. Besides, this cave will make as good a tomb as any."

She turned, her decision final and set out along the path that she had taken with Koldo earlier. They walked for about half an hour when Claire stumbled briefly and reached down to adjust her boot.

"What is it?" Vanguard said.

"Nothing. A stone in my boot. Keep going, I'll catch you up."

Crouched down, she watched as Vanguard and Koldo carried on. Then she stood and followed.

"Stop," she said. "That will do."

They were at the edge of a ravine that dropped sharply away to the left with scrub and bushes. Vanguard turned and stopped dead. Claire held her pistol aimed at his chest.

For a second or two, they stood in a tableau. The mountains were silent apart from the cry of a raptor somewhere overhead.

"This is where it stops, James."

"But..."

"No buts. You were clever, I'll give you that. An SOE agent embedded in the SS, that's a class act. But you made a mistake. Well, two mistakes."

He raised a hand, and she shook her head almost imperceptibly. "Don't even think about it. Take your pistol out of your pocket. Slowly. I am feeling twitchy, so the slower the better." She watched as he complied, lifting the pistol from his pocket with finger and thumb, lifting is so that she could see it clearly, held with the butt up and the barrel pointing to the ground.

"Drop it to the floor and kick it over the ravine."

He did as she ordered without complaint, keeping his hands where she could see them.

"What mistake?"

"The letter. From Otto. That's how I discovered you were Abwehr." She sighed. "I'm sorry. A part of me didn't want to find out." She shrugged. "But here we are. London confirmed it before we left Pau. I had my suspicions, but the letter was the final proof. A careless mistake."

He shook his head. "Not a mistake." His shoulders dropped slightly. "It was his last letter." He sighed, and she saw a vulnerability in him she had never seen before, unlike the fear when he had burst into the Caré Lys Noir a week or so previously. This was different. A deep sadness for a loss that he had never fully recovered from.

"Otto was the father I never had. The father I never knew, my real father, died a long time ago in the trenches. Otto was special. He gave me something that I will always treasure. A purpose."

"And he groomed you for this, for betrayal."

"It depends on which side you are on."

"Does it? You betrayed us, the people who believed you were an ally. You betrayed SOE."

Vanguard nodded. There was no point denying it. Not now. He looked down the ravine. He smiled. He would have chosen this place too. It was ideal. "Mind if I smoke?"

"Don't do anything foolish."

He shook his head, then reached for the cigarette case, running his fingers over it. Alles klar," he said as he lit the cigarette and blew the smoke into the air. "I did not betray Otto or the cause. You said two mistakes."

"You killed them all at the cave," she said. It wasn't a question. "You were in too much of a hurry. Jean-Luc's pistol was placed there, wasn't it?"

"I wanted no witnesses to survive."

"Including me?"

He nodded.

She sighed. "Jean-Luc was your informant for how long?"

He shrugged. "Since I arrived in Rouen. We knew he had a Jewish wife, so he was vulnerable. Why?"

"All that time and you never noticed that he was left-handed?"

He grunted. "In all that time, he usually had his hands in his pockets, wishing he were elsewhere. I never saw him do anything to make that obvious. Still, I suppose we all make mistakes. Some of them are fatal. That's the nature of this game, Claire."

"And you would have killed me when the time was right."

He inclined his head. "Sorry about that."

"Too bad it's the other way around, eh?"

"*Alles Klar*, but Otto would have frowned on my little act of weakness."

She nodded. And pulled the trigger.

She watched as the body tumbled down the scree-lined slope and vanished into the bushes. "*Au revoir, James. Je suis désole.*" She looked at Koldo. "You can go back to Pau, Koldo."

He nodded and headed back the way they had come, and she watched him go.

Chapter 15

Lodève, Present day

François Viala stepped into the office. "I hope I'm not late?"

Clarice looked up from her screen and smiled. "Not at all. You might want to grab a chair from here. It's getting a little crowded in there."

Viala picked up a chair and made his way into the inner office. Clarice was right, he thought. The room was packed. He recognised most of the faces, but two were unfamiliar, and he turned to Clarice, who obliged with introductions. "François Viala, Capitaine, Police Nationale, Montpellier, this is Ingrid Keller, archivist from Berlin, and Geoffrey Spencer, British Intelligence, London. He's the reason we are all here."

Viala nodded a polite greeting and took his seat. The room grew quiet. Spencer stood at the head of the table and looked at the group.

"First," he said, "I apologise if I've caused you any inconvenience."

No one responded. No one in the room was convinced he was at all sorry. Ingrid Keller had been reluctant to travel to Lodève initially, but an all-expenses-paid flight and the promise of a resolution to the mystery had swayed her. Now, like the others, she waited.

"You people gave my organisation quite the run around," Spencer said. "When Monsieur Defrense began asking questions, the ripples reached us quickly. We tried to shut it down, with the help of our French colleagues."

"And they caused his death," Viala said flatly.

Spencer winced. "Yes, Sorry about that, Capitaine. That wasn't supposed to happen. With all due respect to them, they were not to know he was so unwell."

"Go on."

Spencer took a breath. "We hoped the pressure would be enough to make you all back off. But Pascale was, well, let's just say she's as tenacious as her grandmother. As a team, you've done remarkable work. I congratulate you. However…"

"However, what?" Pascale said.

"I now have to shut the investigation down." He raised a hand as voices stirred. "Please. Hear me out."

He paused before continuing. "During the war, SOE and British intelligence more broadly took pride in one thing above all: the belief that the Abwehr never got one over on us. We were humiliated during the Cold War with the Cambridge spies, but our wartime record? That was untouchable."

"Apart from Vanguard," Radfield said.

Spencer nodded. "Apart from Vanguard. My grandfather, Arthur, was tasked with recruiting elite agents. Kerr seemed ideal. A Royal Scots officer, fluent in German, educated, and polished. The information we received from his regiment made him an outstanding candidate for recruitment. Of course, that was Otto Reinhard and his colleagues' plan all along. We knew he'd lived in Germany. That made him valuable as it was with my Grandfather."

"But," Radfield said, "your grandfather didn't look deep enough."

Spencer nodded again, slower this time. "A lapse. One he regretted to the end of his life. Kerr was too good to be true, and we took the bait. Hook, line, and sinker, as they say. They must have been laughing their arses off in Berlin. It's a deep embarrassment. For the service. And for my family. We prefer the truth remain buried."

Pascale sipped her coffee and held Spencer's gaze. "And if we choose to go public?"

"You're within your rights," Spencer said. "Everything you've found is in public archives. You've broken no laws. So… we cannot stop you."

"But you'd rather we didn't."

Spencer leaned back and looked at her as a gambler with a winning hand might look across the poker table. Pascale, a skilled player herself, recognised that look.

"Because, madame, I hold the last piece of your puzzle." He let the bait settle. "You weren't just looking for James Kerr, were you?"

Pascale's voice was quiet as she met his eye. "No. This was always about *Grand-mère*."

He nodded and gave a half smile as he played his ace. "I can tell you where Claire Lemoine is."

The room fell silent.

"Well?" Patrice asked. "What do you want in return?"

"I'm glad you asked." Spencer opened his briefcase and removed a stack of papers. "Copies of the Official Secrets Act. And the French equivalent."

Radfield raised an eyebrow. "And if we sign?"

"You'll get what you came for. Pascale gets to find out what happened to her grandmother. That's the deal."

He looked around the room, one at a time. The silence returned, heavy with unspoken debate. Then Radfield reached for a pen. He signed without hesitation and pushed the papers back to Spencer, who took them with the barest of nods.

Pascale followed, and then Patrice. One by one, each team member signed and pushed the documents across the table.

Spencer gathered them up, his face unreadable.

"Thank you," he said. "Now, let me tell you what happened to Claire Lemoine."

***

Le Cres, Present day.

Pascale switched off the bike, and the engine died into silence. She flicked the sidestand down and rested the machine onto it. For a second or two, she sat there, looking around at the pastoral scene and reflecting on what a contrast it was to the world her grandmother had lived in some eighty years before.

Eventually, she sighed, swung her leg over the saddle, stood and took off her helmet, hanging it on one mirror. Clutching the strap of her bag, she walked up to the front door of her mother's house and rang the bell.

"Maman," she said when Colette opened the door.

"Pascale," she said, kissing her daughter on the cheek. "This is a surprise."

"And I do have a surprise for you, Maman. We need to go inside."

Puzzled by the urgency, Colette led her through to the kitchen, and Pascale sat down. Colette took the coffee pot off the hob and poured two cups. Pascale pulled the letter from her bag and handed it to her mother, who looked at her with raised eyebrows.

"What is this?"

"It's a letter. From *Grand-mère* Claire."

Colette turned it over in her hands. "It's still sealed. Where has it been all this time?"

"In a little café in Rouen, where *Grand-mère* worked as a Resistance agent. She left it for you, but they couldn't find you. They kept it there ever since. In case you ever came by."

"Oh my. I don't know what to do..."

"Open it, I suppose."

"Yes, I suppose."

Carefully, Colette opened the envelope, drew out the letter, and read.

"My dear Colette,

If you are reading this, either I am dead, which is likely, or SOE has extracted me and I have had to disappear.

Things have become complicated by a betrayal. Now, I face a march into the mountains.

As I may never return, I take this opportunity to let you know that you were always loved.

Your father's death means that you are alone in the world now, but the people at SOE have promised to look after you, and I trust they will keep their word.

When I left you, I did so with a heavy heart. And it is still heavy, but I had to do my duty. The world is a dark place right now, and if ordinary people cannot make the necessary sacrifices, then the shadow over Europe will remain.

I am doing what I can for France, and by extension, for you. I hope that one day, you will find it in your heart to forgive me.

With all of my love, always,

Your loving mother,

Claire Lemoine.

Vive la France."

Colette handed the letter to Pascale, who read it silently. When she looked up, her voice was quiet, and she could barely see.

"Well, now we know," she said.

***

Leatherhead, Surrey, Present Day

"I always liked the view of the Oxshott woods," Linda Samson said as she looked at the view, leaning on her stick. "I used to look out across at them from the classroom. "This place was a school once, you know."

"Then," said the carer, "let's get you to your favourite bench." She reached out to take the old woman's arm.

"I'm old, not infirm," Linda said. "I don't need mollycoddling, young woman," she said, tapping her stick sharply on the ground.

The carer smiled and walked alongside Linda as she moved carefully, using the stick to aid her balance. They arrived at the bench under a walnut tree, and Linda sat, resting the stick alongside her.

"Do you want a blanket?" the carer asked. Linda glared up at her. "I'll take that as a no, shall I?"

"Indeed, you shall. I've killed people, you know. It might have been a long time ago, but I haven't forgotten how."

"Of course you have, dear. Well, I'll leave you to it, then."

She walked away, shaking her head and smiling. Another member of staff joined her as they walked back into the building. "She's killed people, you know," she said with a smile.

Linda pretended not to have heard them as she looked across at a scene she had enjoyed since her twenties. She must have dozed off, and the past drifted into her dreams again—the old cell from so long ago, the forced march through the mountains, and the final shot. She awoke with a start.

"Miss Samson, you have visitors."

"Visitors? Pah! Everyone I know is dead. I don't need visitors."

She turned to look at the two women. She frowned slightly. "Do I know you?"

"Hello, Flamme," Pascale said.

Claire widened her eyes as she looked at them, one to the other, not quite believing what she saw.

"My word! I've not been called that name for a long time." She frowned. "Who are you people?"

"Hello, Maman," Collete said.

"Colette? Colette, is it really you?"

"Yes, Maman. I waited for so long..." She dropped to her knees to embrace Claire. "And you are?" Claire said, looking up at Pascale as she embraced her daughter.

"Pascale, Hervé *Grand-mère*. "I've been waiting for this moment, too."

She turned and looked back at the building where Geneviève stood, lounging against the wall. She lifted a finger to her brow in a salute and winked.

About the author

Mark Ellott is a writer of historical thrillers and supernatural horror, blending meticulous research with gripping storytelling. With a keen interest in espionage, wartime deception, and folklore, his works explore the shadows of history and the unknown. His stories often feature complex protagonists navigating dangerous worlds, where truth and identity are never quite what they seem.

Recently retired from a career in railway operations, Mark now devotes his time to writing and his love of motorcycling. When not at his desk, he can be found exploring historical sites, delving into archives, or contemplating his next unsettling twist. He believes the best stories linger long after the final page—whether through a chilling revelation or a question left unanswered.

Printed in Dunstable, United Kingdom